GO!

with

Outlook 2007

Getting Started

Shelley Gaskin and Kris Townsend

PEARSON

Prentice
Hall

Upper Saddle River, New Jersey

This book is dedicated to my students, who inspire me every day, and to my husband, Fred Gaskin.
—Shelley Gaskin

This book is dedicated to my two moms, Janice and Norma.
—Kris Townsend

Library of Congress Cataloging-in-Publication Data

Gaskin, Shelley.
Go! Getting started with Outlook 7.0 / Shelley Gaskin and Kris Townsend.
    p. cm.
Includes index.
ISBN 0-13-225617-7
1. Microsoft Outlook. 2. Time management--Computer programs. 3. Personal information management--Computer programs. I. Townsend, Kris. II. Title. III. Title: Getting started with Outlook 7.0.
HF5548.4.M5255G37 2008
005.5'7--dc22

2007009640

Vice President and Publisher: Natalie E. Anderson
Associate VP/Executive Acquisitions Editor, Print: Stephanie Wall
Executive Acquisitions Editor, Media: Richard Keaveny
Product Development Manager: Eileen Bien Calabro Sr.
Editorial Project Manager: Laura Burgess
Development Editor: Ginny Munroe
Editorial Assistants: Becky Knauer, Lora Cimiluca
Content Development Manager: Cathi Profitko
Production Media Project Manager: Lorena Cerisano
Senior Media Project Manager: Steve Gagliostro
Director of Marketing: Margaret Waples
Senior Marketing Manager: Jason Sakos
Sales Associate: Rebecca Scott
Managing Editor: Lynda J. Castillo

Production Project Manager/Buyer: Wanda Rockwell
Production Editor: GGS Book Services
Photo Researcher: GGS Book Services
Manufacturing Buyer: Natacha Moore
Production/Editorial Assistant: Sandra K. Bernales
Design Director: Maria Lange
Art Director/Interior Design: Blair Brown
Cover Photo: Courtesy of Getty Images, Inc./Marvin Mattelson
Composition: GGS Book Services
Project Management: GGS Book Services
Cover Printer: Phoenix Color
Printer/Binder: Courier

Microsoft, Windows, Word, PowerPoint, Outlook, FrontPage, Visual Basic, MSN, The Microsoft Network, and/or other Microsoft products referenced herein are either trademarks or registered trademarks of Microsoft Corporation in the U.S.A. and other countries. Screen shots and icons reprinted with permission from the Microsoft Corporation. This book is not sponsored or endorsed by or affiliated with Microsoft Corporation.

Credits and acknowledgments borrowed from other sources and reproduced, with permission, in this textbook are as follows or on the appropriate page within the text.

    Page 2: Getty Images, Inc.

10 9
ISBN-10: 0-13-225617-7
ISBN-13: 978-0-13-225617-9

Table of Contents

Letter from the Editor

Dear Instructors and Students,

The primary goal of the *GO!* Series is two-fold. The first goal is to help instructors teach the course they want in less time. The second goal is to provide students with the skills to solve business problems using the computer as a tool, for both themselves and the organization for which they might be employed.

The *GO!* Series was originally created by Series Editor Shelley Gaskin and published with the release of Microsoft Office 2003. Her ideas came from years of using textbooks that didn't meet all the needs of today's diverse classroom and that were too confusing for students. Shelley continues to enhance the series by ensuring we stay true to our vision of developing quality instruction and useful classroom tools.

But we also need your input and ideas.

Over time, the *GO!* Series has evolved based on direct feedback from instructors and students using the series. *We are the publisher that listens.* To publish a textbook that works for you, it's critical that we continue to listen to this feedback. It's important to me to talk with you and hear your stories about using *GO!* Your voice can make a difference.

My hope is that this letter will inspire you to write me an e-mail and share your thoughts on using the *GO!* Series.

Stephanie Wall
Executive Editor, *GO!* Series
stephanie_wall@prenhall.com

GO! System Contributors

We thank the following people for their hard work and support in making the GO! System all that it is!

Additional Author Support

Coyle, Diane	Montgomery County Community College
Fry, Susan	Boise State
Townsend, Kris	Spokane Falls Community College
Stroup, Tracey	Amgen Corporation

Instructor Resource Authors

Amer, Beverly	Northern Arizona University	Paterson, Jim	Paradise Valley Community College
Boito, Nancy	Harrisburg Area Community College	Prince, Lisa	Missouri State
Coyle, Diane	Montgomery County Community College	Rodgers, Gwen	Southern Nazarene University
Dawson, Tamara	Southern Nazarene University	Ruymann, Amy	Burlington Community College
Driskel, Loretta	Niagara County Community College	Ryan, Bob	Montgomery County Community College
Elliott, Melissa	Odessa College		
Fry, Susan	Boise State	Smith, Diane	Henry Ford College
Geoghan, Debra	Bucks County Community College	Spangler, Candice	Columbus State Community College
Hearn, Barbara	Community College of Philadelphia	Thompson, Joyce	Lehigh Carbon Community College
Jones, Stephanie	South Plains College	Tiffany, Janine	Reading Area Community College
Madsen, Donna	Kirkwood Community College	Watt, Adrienne	Douglas College
Meck, Kari	Harrisburg Area Community College	Weaver, Paul	Bossier Parish Community College
Miller, Cindy	Ivy Tech	Weber, Sandy	Gateway Technical College
Nowakowski, Tony	Buffalo State	Wood, Dawn	
Pace, Phyllis	Queensborough Community College	Weissman, Jonathan	Finger Lakes Community College

Super Reviewers

Brotherton, Cathy	Riverside Community College	Maurer, Trina	Odessa College
Cates, Wally	Central New Mexico Community College	Meck, Kari	Harrisburg Area Community College
		Miller, Cindy	Ivy Tech Community College
Cone, Bill	Northern Arizona University	Nielson, Phil	Salt Lake Community College
Coverdale, John	Riverside Community College	Rodgers, Gwen	Southern Nazarene University
Foster, Nancy	Baker College	Smolenski, Robert	Delaware Community College
Helfand, Terri	Chaffey College	Spangler, Candice	Columbus State Community College
Hibbert, Marilyn	Salt Lake Community College	Thompson, Joyce	Lehigh Carbon Community College
Holliday, Mardi	Community College of Philadelphia	Weber, Sandy	Gateway Technical College
Jerry, Gina	Santa Monica College	Wells, Lorna	Salt Lake Community College
Martin, Carol	Harrisburg Area Community College	Zaboski, Maureen	University of Scranton

Technical Editors

Janice Snyder
Joyce Nielsen
Colette Eisele
Janet Pickard
Mara Zebest
Lindsey Allen
William Daley

Student Reviewers

Allen, John	Asheville-Buncombe Tech Community College	Erickson, Mike	Ball State University
		Gadomski, Amanda	Northern Michigan University
Alexander, Steven	St. Johns River Community College	Gyselinck, Craig	Central Washington University
Alexander, Melissa	Tulsa Community College	Harrison, Margo	Central Washington University
Bolz, Stephanie	Northern Michigan University	Heacox, Kate	Central Washington University
Berner, Ashley	Central Washington University	Hill, Cheretta	Northwestern State University
Boomer, Michelle	Northern Michigan University	Innis, Tim	Tulsa Community College
Busse, Brennan	Northern Michigan University	Jarboe, Aaron	Central Washington University
Butkey, Maura	Central Washington University	Klein, Colleen	Northern Michigan University
Christensen, Kaylie	Northern Michigan University	Moeller, Jeffrey	Northern Michigan University
Connally, Brianna	Central Washington University	Nicholson, Regina	Athens Tech College
Davis, Brandon	Northern Michigan University	Niehaus, Kristina	Northern Michigan University
Davis, Christen	Central Washington University	Nisa, Zaibun	Santa Rosa Community College
Den Boer, Lance	Central Washington University	Nunez, Nohelia	Santa Rosa Community College
Dix, Jessica	Central Washington University	Oak, Samantha	Central Washington University
Moeller, Jeffrey	Northern Michigan University	Oertii, Monica	Central Washington University
Downs, Elizabeth	Central Washington University	Palenshus, Juliet	Central Washington University

Pohl, Amanda	Northern Michigan University	Shanahan, Megan	Northern Michigan University
Presnell, Randy	Central Washington University	Teska, Erika	Hawaii Pacific University
Ritner, April	Northern Michigan University	Traub, Amy	Northern Michigan University
Rodriguez, Flavia	Northwestern State University	Underwood, Katie	Central Washington University
Roberts, Corey	Tulsa Community College	Walters, Kim	Central Washington University
Rossi, Jessica Ann	Central Washington University	Wilson, Kelsie	Central Washington University
Shafapay, Natasha	Central Washington University	Wilson, Amanda	Green River Community College

Series Reviewers

Abraham, Reni	Houston Community College	Crawford, Thomasina	Miami-Dade College, Kendall Campus
Agatston, Ann	Agatston Consulting Technical College	Credico, Grace	Lethbridge Community College
Alexander, Melody	Ball Sate University	Crenshaw, Richard	Miami Dade Community College, North
Alejandro, Manuel	Southwest Texas Junior College	Crespo, Beverly	Mt. San Antonio College
Ali, Farha	Lander University	Crossley, Connie	Cincinnati State Technical Community College
Amici, Penny	Harrisburg Area Community College	Curik, Mary	Central New Mexico Community College
Anderson, Patty A.	Lake City Community College		
Andrews, Wilma	Virginia Commonwealth College, Nebraska University	De Arazoza, Ralph	Miami Dade Community College
Anik, Mazhar	Tiffin University	Danno, John	DeVry University/Keller Graduate School
Armstrong, Gary	Shippensburg University	Davis, Phillip	Del Mar College
Atkins, Bonnie	Delaware Technical Community College	DeHerrera, Laurie	Pikes Peak Community College
Bachand, LaDonna	Santa Rosa Community College	Delk, Dr. K. Kay	Seminole Community College
Bagui, Sikha	University of West Florida	Doroshow, Mike	Eastfield College
Beecroft, Anita	Kwantlen University College	Douglas, Gretchen	SUNYCortland
Bell, Paula	Lock Haven College	Dove, Carol	Community College of Allegheny
Belton, Linda	Springfield Tech. Community College	Driskel, Loretta	Niagara Community College
		Duckwiler, Carol	Wabaunsee Community College
Bennett, Judith	Sam Houston State University	Duncan, Mimi	University of Missouri-St. Louis
Bhatia, Sai	Riverside Community College	Duthie, Judy	Green River Community College
Bishop, Frances	DeVry Institute—Alpharetta (ATL)	Duvall, Annette	Central New Mexico Community College
Blaszkiewicz, Holly	Ivy Tech Community College/Region 1		
Branigan, Dave	DeVry University	Ecklund, Paula	Duke University
Bray, Patricia	Allegany College of Maryland	Eng, Bernice	Brookdale Community College
Brotherton, Cathy	Riverside Community College	Evans, Billie	Vance-Granville Community College
Buehler, Lesley	Ohlone College	Feuerbach, Lisa	Ivy Tech East Chicago
Buell, C	Central Oregon Community College	Fisher, Fred	Florida State University
Byars, Pat	Brookhaven College	Foster, Penny L.	Anne Arundel Community College
Byrd, Lynn	Delta State University, Cleveland, Mississippi	Foszcz, Russ	McHenry County College
		Fry, Susan	Boise State University
Cacace, Richard N.	Pensacola Junior College	Fustos, Janos	Metro State
Cadenhead, Charles	Brookhaven College	Gallup, Jeanette	Blinn College
Calhoun, Ric	Gordon College	Gelb, Janet	Grossmont College
Cameron, Eric	Passaic Community College	Gentry, Barb	Parkland College
Carriker, Sandra	North Shore Community College	Gerace, Karin	St. Angela Merici School
Cannamore, Madie	Kennedy King	Gerace, Tom	Tulane University
Carreon, Cleda	Indiana University—Purdue University, Indianapolis	Ghajar, Homa	Oklahoma State University
		Gifford, Steve	Northwest Iowa Community College
Chaffin, Catherine	Shawnee State University	Glazer, Ellen	Broward Community College
Chauvin, Marg	Palm Beach Community College, Boca Raton	Gordon, Robert	Hofstra University
		Gramlich, Steven	Pasco-Hernando Community College
Challa, Chandrashekar	Virginia State University	Graviett, Nancy M.	St. Charles Community College, St. Peters, Missouri
Chamlou, Afsaneh	NOVA Alexandria		
Chapman, Pam	Wabaunsee Community College	Greene, Rich	Community College of Allegheny County
Christensen, Dan	Iowa Western Community College		
Clay, Betty	Southeastern Oklahoma State University	Gregoryk, Kerry	Virginia Commonwealth State
		Griggs, Debra	Bellevue Community College
Collins, Linda D.	Mesa Community College	Grimm, Carol	Palm Beach Community College
Conroy-Link, Janet	Holy Family College	Hahn, Norm	Thomas Nelson Community College
Cosgrove, Janet	Northwestern CT Community	Hammerschlag, Dr. Bill	Brookhaven College
Courtney, Kevin	Hillsborough Community College	Hansen, Michelle	Davenport University
Cox, Rollie	Madison Area Technical College	Hayden, Nancy	Indiana University—Purdue University, Indianapolis
Crawford, Hiram	Olive Harvey College		

Hayes, Theresa	Broward Community College	Lord, Alexandria	Asheville Buncombe Tech
Helfand, Terri	Chaffey College	Lowe, Rita	Harold Washington College
Helms, Liz	Columbus State Community College	Low, Willy Hui	Joliet Junior College
Hernandez, Leticia	TCI College of Technology	Lucas, Vickie	Broward Community College
Hibbert, Marilyn	Salt Lake Community College	Lynam, Linda	Central Missouri State University
Hoffman, Joan	Milwaukee Area Technical College	Lyon, Lynne	Durham College
Hogan, Pat	Cape Fear Community College	Lyon, Pat Rajski	Tomball College
Holland, Susan	Southeast Community College	MacKinnon, Ruth	Georgia Southern University
Hopson, Bonnie	Athens Technical College	Macon, Lisa	Valencia Community College, West Campus
Horvath, Carrie	Albertus Magnus College		
Horwitz, Steve	Community College of Philadelphia	Machuca, Wayne	College of the Sequoias
Hotta, Barbara	Leeward Community College	Madison, Dana	Clarion University
Howard, Bunny	St. Johns River Community	Maguire, Trish	Eastern New Mexico University
Howard, Chris	DeVry University	Malkan, Rajiv	Montgomery College
Huckabay, Jamie	Austin Community College	Manning, David	Northern Kentucky University
Hudgins, Susan	East Central University	Marcus, Jacquie	Niagara Community College
Hulett, Michelle J.	Missouri State University	Marghitu, Daniela	Auburn University
Hunt, Darla A.	Morehead State University, Morehead, Kentucky	Marks, Suzanne	Bellevue Community College
		Marquez, Juanita	El Centro College
Hunt, Laura	Tulsa Community College	Marquez, Juan	Mesa Community College
Jacob, Sherry	Jefferson Community College	Martyn, Margie	Baldwin-Wallace College
Jacobs, Duane	Salt Lake Community College	Marucco, Toni	Lincoln Land Community College
Jauken, Barb	Southeastern Community	Mason, Lynn	Lubbock Christian University
Johnson, Kathy	Wright College	Matutis, Audrone	Houston Community College
Johnson, Mary	Kingwood College	Matkin, Marie	University of Lethbridge
Johnson, Mary	Mt. San Antonio College	McCain, Evelynn	Boise State University
Jones, Stacey	Benedict College	McCannon, Melinda	Gordon College
Jones, Warren	University of Alabama, Birmingham	McCarthy, Marguerite	Northwestern Business College
Jordan, Cheryl	San Juan College	McCaskill, Matt L.	Brevard Community College
Kapoor, Bhushan	California State University, Fullerton	McClellan, Carolyn	Tidewater Community College
Kasai, Susumu	Salt Lake Community College	McClure, Darlean	College of Sequoias
Kates, Hazel	Miami Dade Community College, Kendall	McCrory, Sue A.	Missouri State University
		McCue, Stacy	Harrisburg Area Community College
Keen, Debby	University of Kentucky	McEntire-Orbach, Teresa	Middlesex County College
Keeter, Sandy	Seminole Community College	McLeod, Todd	Fresno City College
Kern-Blystone, Dorothy Jean	Bowling Green State	McManus, Illyana	Grossmont College
		McPherson, Dori	Schoolcraft College
Keskin, Ilknur	The University of South Dakota	Meiklejohn, Nancy	Pikes Peak Community College
Kirk, Colleen	Mercy College	Menking, Rick	Hardin-Simmons University
Kleckner, Michelle	Elon University	Meredith, Mary	University of Louisiana at Lafayette
Kliston, Linda	Broward Community College, North Campus	Mermelstein, Lisa	Baruch College
		Metos, Linda	Salt Lake Community College
Kochis, Dennis	Suffolk County Community College	Meurer, Daniel	University of Cincinnati
Kramer, Ed	Northern Virginia Community College	Meyer, Marian	Central New Mexico Community College
Laird, Jeff	Northeast State Community College	Miller, Cindy	Ivy Tech Community College, Lafayette, Indiana
Lamoureaux, Jackie	Central New Mexico Community College		
		Mitchell, Susan	Davenport University
Lange, David	Grand Valley State	Mohle, Dennis	Fresno Community College
LaPointe, Deb	Central New Mexico Community College	Monk, Ellen	University of Delaware
		Moore, Rodney	Holland College
Larson, Donna	Louisville Technical Institute	Morris, Mike	Southeastern Oklahoma State University
Laspina, Kathy	Vance-Granville Community College		
Le Grand, Dr. Kate	Broward Community College	Morris, Nancy	Hudson Valley Community College
Lenhart, Sheryl	Terra Community College	Moseler, Dan	Harrisburg Area Community College
Letavec, Chris	University of Cincinnati	Nabors, Brent	Reedley College, Clovis Center
Liefert, Jane	Everett Community College	Nadas, Erika	Wright College
Lindaman, Linda	Black Hawk Community College	Nadelman, Cindi	New England College
Lindberg, Martha	Minnesota State University	Nademlynsky, Lisa	Johnson & Wales University
Lightner, Renee	Broward Community College	Ncube, Cathy	University of West Florida
Lindberg, Martha	Minnesota State University	Nagengast, Joseph	Florida Career College
Linge, Richard	Arizona Western College	Newsome, Eloise	Northern Virginia Community College Woodbridge
Logan, Mary G.	Delgado Community College		
Loizeaux, Barbara	Westchester Community College	Nicholls, Doreen	Mohawk Valley Community College
Lopez, Don	Clovis-State Center Community College District	Nunan, Karen	Northeast State Technical Community College

Odegard, Teri	Edmonds Community College	Sterling, Janet	Houston Community College
Ogle, Gregory	North Community College	Stoughton, Catherine	Laramie County Community College
Orr, Dr. Claudia	Northern Michigan University South	Sullivan, Angela	Joliet Junior College
Otieno, Derek	DeVry University	Szurek, Joseph	University of Pittsburgh at Greensburg
Otton, Diana Hill	Chesapeake College		
Oxendale, Lucia	West Virginia Institute of Technology	Tarver, Mary Beth	Northwestern State University
		Taylor, Michael	Seattle Central Community College
Paiano, Frank	Southwestern College	Thangiah, Sam	Slippery Rock University
Patrick, Tanya	Clackamas Community College	Thompson-Sellers, Ingrid	Georgia Perimeter College
Peairs, Deb	Clark State Community College	Tomasi, Erik	Baruch College
Prince, Lisa	Missouri State University-Springfield Campus	Toreson, Karen	Shoreline Community College
		Trifiletti, John J.	Florida Community College at Jacksonville
Proietti, Kathleen	Northern Essex Community College		
Pusins, Delores	HCCC	Trivedi, Charulata	Quinsigamond Community College, Woodbridge
Raghuraman, Ram	Joliet Junior College		
Reasoner, Ted Allen	Indiana University—Purdue	Tucker, William	Austin Community College
Reeves, Karen	High Point University	Turgeon, Cheryl	Asnuntuck Community College
Remillard, Debbie	New Hampshire Technical Institute	Turpen, Linda	Central New Mexico Community College
Rhue, Shelly	DeVry University		
Richards, Karen	Maplewoods Community College	Upshaw, Susan	Del Mar College
Richardson, Mary	Albany Technical College	Unruh, Angela	Central Washington University
Rodgers, Gwen	Southern Nazarene University	Vanderhoof, Dr. Glenna	Missouri State University-Springfield Campus
Roselli, Diane	Harrisburg Area Community College		
Ross, Dianne	University of Louisiana in Lafayette	Vargas, Tony	El Paso Community College
Rousseau, Mary	Broward Community College, South	Vicars, Mitzi	Hampton University
Samson, Dolly	Hawaii Pacific University	Villarreal, Kathleen	Fresno
Sams, Todd	University of Cincinnati	Vitrano, Mary Ellen	Palm Beach Community College
Sandoval, Everett	Reedley College	Volker, Bonita	Tidewater Community College
Sardone, Nancy	Seton Hall University	Wahila, Lori (Mindy)	Tompkins Cortland Community College
Scafide, Jean	Mississippi Gulf Coast Community College		
		Waswick, Kim	Southeast Community College, Nebraska
Scheeren, Judy	Westmoreland County Community College		
		Wavle, Sharon	Tompkins Cortland Community College
Schneider, Sol	Sam Houston State University		
Scroggins, Michael	Southwest Missouri State University	Webb, Nancy	City College of San Francisco
Sever, Suzanne	Northwest Arkansas Community College	Wells, Barbara E.	Central Carolina Technical College
		Wells, Lorna	Salt Lake Community College
Sheridan, Rick	California State University-Chico	Welsh, Jean	Lansing Community College Nebraska
Silvers, Pamela	Asheville Buncombe Tech		
Singer, Steven A.	University of Hawai'i, Kapi'olani Community College	White, Bruce	Quinnipiac University
		Willer, Ann	Solano Community College
Sinha, Atin	Albany State University	Williams, Mark	Lane Community College
Skolnick, Martin	Florida Atlantic University	Wilson, Kit	Red River College
Smith, T. Michael	Austin Community College	Wilson, Roger	Fairmont State University
Smith, Tammy	Tompkins Cortland Community Collge	Wimberly, Leanne	International Academy of Design and Technology
Smolenski, Bob	Delaware County Community College	Worthington, Paula	Northern Virginia Community College
Spangler, Candice	Columbus State		
Stedham, Vicki	St. Petersburg College, Clearwater	Yauney, Annette	Herkimer County Community College
Stefanelli, Greg	Carroll Community College		
Steiner, Ester	New Mexico State University	Yip, Thomas	Passaic Community College
Stenlund, Neal	Northern Virginia Community College, Alexandria	Zavala, Ben	Webster Tech
		Zlotow, Mary Ann	College of DuPage
St. John, Steve	Tulsa Community College	Zudeck, Steve	Broward Community College, North

About the Authors

Shelley Gaskin, Series Editor, is a professor of business and computer technology at Pasadena City College in Pasadena, California. She holds a master's degree in business education from Northern Illinois University and a doctorate in adult and community education from Ball State University. Dr. Gaskin has 15 years of experience in the computer industry with several Fortune 500 companies and has developed and written training materials for custom systems applications in both the public and private sector. She is also the author of books on Microsoft Outlook and word processing.

Kris Townsend is an information systems instructor and department chair at Spokane Falls Community College in Spokane, Washington, where he teaches computer applications, Internet programming, and digital forensics. Kris received a bachelor's in education and a bachelor's in business from Eastern Washington University with majors in mathematics and management information systems, respectively. He received his master's in education from City University with an emphasis in educational technology. Kris has also worked as a public school teacher and as a systems analyst for a public school assessment department.

In addition to teaching and authoring, Kris enjoys working with wood, snowboarding, and camping. He commutes to work by bike and enjoys long road rides in the Palouse country south of Spokane.

Visual Walk-Through of the *GO!* System

The *GO!* System is designed for ease of implementation on the instructor side and ease of understanding on the student. It has been completely developed based on professor and student feedback.

The *GO!* System is divided into three categories that reflect how you might organize your course— **Prepare**, **Teach**, and **Assess**.

Prepare

GO!

Because the GO! System was designed and written by instructors like yourself, it includes the tools that allow you to Prepare, Teach, and Assess in your course. We have organized the GO! System into these three categories that match how you work through your course and thus, it's even easier for you to implement.

To help you get started, here is an outline of the first activities you may want to do in order to conduct your course.

There are several other tools not listed here that are available in the GO! System so please refer to your GO! Guide for a complete listing of all the tools.

Prepare
1. Prepare the course syllabus
2. Plan the course assignments
3. Organize the student resources

Teach
4. Conduct demonstrations and lectures

Assess
5. Assign and grade assignments, quizzes, tests, and assessments

PREPARE

1. Prepare the course syllabus

A syllabus template is provided on the IRCD in the **go07_syllabus_template** folder of the main directory. It includes a course calendar planner for 8-week, 12-week, and 16-week formats. Depending on your term (summer or regular semester) you can modify one of these according to your course plan, and then add information pertinent to your course and institution.

2. Plan course assignments

For each chapter, an Assignment Sheet listing every in-chapter and end-of-chapter project is located on the IRCD within the **go01_gotoffice2007intro_instructor_resources_by_chapter** folder. From there, navigate to the specific chapter folder. These sheets are Word tables, so you can delete rows for the projects that you choose not to assign or add rows for your own assignments—if any. There is a column to add the number of points you want to assign to each project depending on your grading scheme. At the top of the sheet, you can fill in the course information.

Transitioning to GO! Office 2007 — Page 1 of 1

NEW

Transition Guide

New to *GO!*–We've made it quick and easy to plan the format and activities for your class.

Syllabus Template

Includes course calendar planner for 8-, 12-, and 16-week formats.

GO! with Microsoft Office 2007 Introductory
SAMPLE SYLLABUS (16 weeks)

I. COURSE INFORMATION

Course No.:	Semester:
Course Title:	Credits:
Course Hours:	

Instructor:	Office:
Office Hours:	
Email:	Phone:

II. TEXT AND MATERIALS

Before starting the course, you will need the following:

- GO! with Microsoft Office 2007 Introductory by Shelley Gaskin, Robert L. Ferrett, Alicia Vargas, Suzanne Marks ©2007, published by Pearson Prentice Hall. ISBN 0-13-167990-6
- Storage device for saving files (any of the following: multiple diskettes, CD-RW, flash drive, etc.)

III. WHAT YOU WILL LEARN IN THIS COURSE

This is a hands-on course where you will learn to use a computer to practice the most commonly used Microsoft programs including the Windows operating system, Internet Explorer for navigating the Internet, Outlook for managing your personal information and the four most popular programs within the Microsoft Office Suite (Word, Excel, PowerPoint and Access). You will also practice the basics of using a computer, mouse and keyboard. You will learn to be an intermediate level user of the Microsoft Office Suite.

Within the Microsoft Office Suite, you will use Word, Excel, PowerPoint, and Access. Microsoft Word is a word processing program with which you can create common business and personal documents. Microsoft Excel is a spreadsheet program that organizes and calculates accounting-type information. Microsoft PowerPoint is a presentation graphics program with which you can develop slides to accompany an oral presentation. Finally, Microsoft Access is a database program that organizes large amounts of information in a useful manner.

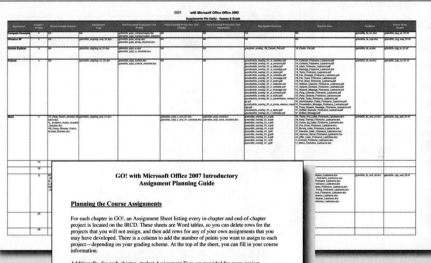

Assignment Sheet

One per chapter. Lists all possible assignments; add to and delete from this simple Word table according to your course plan.

File Guide to the GO! Supplements

Tabular listing of all supplements and their file names.

NEW

Assignment Planning Guide

Description of GO! assignments with recommendations based on class size, delivery mode, and student needs. Includes examples from fellow instructors.

GO! with Microsoft Office 2007 Introductory Assignment Planning Guide

Planning the Course Assignments

For each chapter in GO!, an Assignment Sheet listing every in-chapter and end-of-chapter project is located on the IRCD. These sheets are Word tables, so you can delete rows for the projects that you will not assign, and then add rows for any of your own assignments that you may have developed. There is a column to add the number of points you want to assign to each project—depending on your grading scheme. At the top of the sheet, you can fill in your course information.

Additionally, for each chapter, student Assignment Tags are provided for every project (including Problem Solving projects)—also located on the IRCD. These are small scoring checklists on which you can check off errors made by the student, and with which the student can verify that all project elements are complete. For campus classes, the student can attach the tags to his or her paper submissions. For online classes, many GO! instructors have the student include these with the electronic submission.

Deciding What to Assign

Front Portion of the Chapter—Instructional Projects: The projects in the front portion of the chapter, which are listed on the first page of each chapter, are the instructional projects. Most instructors assign all of these projects, because this is where the student receives the instruction and engages in the active learning.

End-of-Chapter—Practice and Critical Thinking Projects: In the back portion of the chapter (the gray pages), you can assign on a prescriptive basis; that is, for students who were challenged by the instructional projects, you might assign one or more projects from the two *Skills Reviews*, which provide maximum prompting and a thorough review of the entire chapter. For students who have previous software knowledge and who completed the instructional projects easily, you might assign only the *Mastery Projects*.

You can also assign prescriptively by Objective, because each end-of-chapter project indicates the Objectives covered. So you might assign, on a student-by-student basis, only the projects that cover the Objectives with which the student seemed to have difficulty in the instructional projects.

The five Problem Solving projects and the You and GO! project are the authentic assessments that pull together the student's learning. Here the student is presented with a "messy real-life situation" and then uses his or her knowledge and skill to solve a problem, produce a product, give a presentation, or demonstrate a procedure. You might assign one or more of the Problem

GO! Assignment Planning Guide   Page 1 of 1

Student Data Files

Music School Records discovers, launches, and and develops the careers of young artists in classical, jazz, and contemporary music. Our philosophy is to not only shape, distribute, and sell a music product, but to help artists create a career that can lats a lifetime. too often in the music industry, artists are forced to fit their music to a trend that is short-lived. Music School Records doesn't just follow trends, we take a long-term view of the music industry and help our artists develop a style and repertoire that is fluid and flexible and that will appeal to audiences for years and even decades.

The music industry is constantly changing, but over the last decade the changes have been enormous. New forms of entertainment such as DVDs, video games, and the Internet mean there are more competition for the leisure dollar in the market. New technologies give consomers more options for buying and listening to music, and they are demaning high quality recordings. Young consumers are comfortable with technology and want the music they love when and where they want it, no matter where they are or what they are doing.

Music School Records embraces new technologies and the sophisticated market of young music lovers. We believe that providing high quality recordings of truly talented artists make for more discerning listeners who will cherish the gift of music for the rest of their lives. The expertise of Music School Records includes:

- Insight into our target market and the ability to reach the desired audience
- The ability to access all current sources of music income
- A management team with years of experience in music commerce
- Innovative business strategies and artist development plans
- Investment in technology infrastructure for high quality recordings and business services
- Initiative and proactive management of artist careers

Online Study Guide for Students

Interactive objective-style questions based on chapter content.

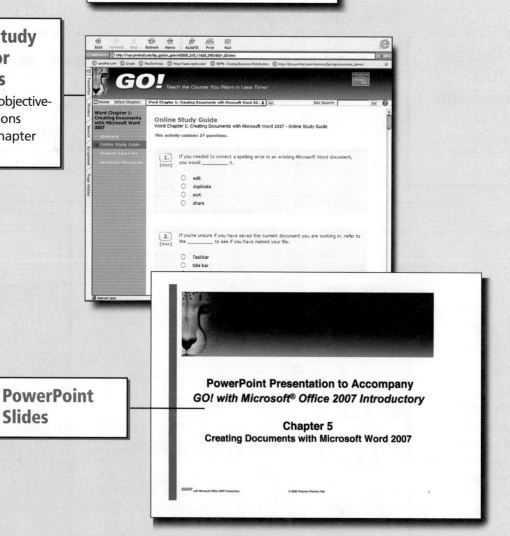

PowerPoint Slides

Teach

Student Textbook

Learning Objectives and Student Outcomes

Objectives are clustered around projects that result in student outcomes. They help students learn how to solve problems, not just learn software features.

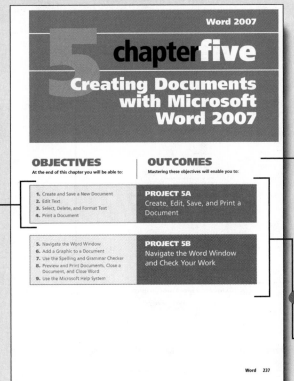

Word 2007

5 chapterfive

Creating Documents with Microsoft Word 2007

OBJECTIVES
At the end of this chapter you will be able to:

OUTCOMES
Mastering these objectives will enable you to:

1. Create and Save a New Document
2. Edit Text
3. Select, Delete, and Format Text
4. Print a Document

PROJECT 5A
Create, Edit, Save, and Print a Document

5. Navigate the Word Window
6. Add a Graphic to a Document
7. Use the Spelling and Grammar Checker
8. Preview and Print Documents, Close a Document, and Close Word
9. Use the Microsoft Help System

PROJECT 5B
Navigate the Word Window and Check Your Work

Project-Based Instruction

Students do not practice features of the application; they create real projects that they will need in the real world. Projects are color coded for easy reference and are named to reflect skills the students will be practicing.

NEW

A and B Projects

Each chapter contains two instructional projects—A and B.

Music School Records

Music School Records was created to launch young musical artists with undiscovered talent in jazz, classical, and contemporary music. The creative management team searches internationally for talented young people, and has a reputation for mentoring and developing the skills of its artists. The company's music is tailored to an audience that is young, knowledgeable about music, and demands the highest quality recordings. Music School Records releases are available in CD format as well as digital downloads.

Getting Started with Microsoft Office Word 2007

A word processor is the most common program found on personal computers and one that almost everyone has a reason to use. When you learn word processing you are also learning skills and techniques that you need to work efficiently on a personal computer. You can use Microsoft Word to perform basic word processing tasks such as writing a memo, a report, or a letter. You can also use Word to complete complex word processing tasks, such as those that include sophisticated tables, embedded graphics, and links to other documents and the Internet. Word is a program that you can learn gradually, and then add more advanced skills one at a time.

Each chapter opens with a story that sets the stage for the projects the student will create; the instruction does not force the student to pretend to be someone or make up a scenario.

Each chapter has an introductory paragraph that briefs students on what is important.

Visual Summary

Shows students upfront what their projects will look like when they are done.

Project Summary

Stated clearly and quickly in one paragraph.

NEW

File Guide

Clearly shows students which files are needed for the project and the names they will use to save their documents.

Objective

The skills the student will learn are clearly stated at the beginning of each project and color coded to match projects listed on the chapter opener page.

NEW

Screen Shots

Larger screen shots.

GO! KEY FEATURE

Teachable Moment

Expository text is woven into the steps—at the moment students need to know it—not chunked together in a block of text that will go unread.

Steps

Color coded to the current project, easy to read, and not too many to confuse the student or too few to be meaningless.

KEY FEATURE

GO! **Sequential Pagination**

No more confusing letters and abbreviations.

Press Enter two more times.

In a business letter, insert two blank lines between the date and the inside address, which is the same as the address you would use on an envelope.

Type **Mr. William Hawken** and then press Enter.

The wavy red line under the proper name *Hawken* indicates that the word has been flagged as misspelled because it is a word not contained in the Word dictionary.

On two lines, type the following address, but do not press Enter at the end of the second line:

123 Eighth Street
Harrisville, MI 48740

Note — Typing the Address

Include a comma after the city name in an inside address. However, for mailing addresses on envelopes, eliminate the comma after the city name.

On the **Home tab**, in the **Styles group**, click the **Normal** button.

The Normal style is applied to the text in the rest of the document. Recall that the Normal style adds extra space between paragraphs; it also adds slightly more space between lines in a paragraph.

Press Enter. Type **Dear William:** and then press Enter.

This salutation is the line that greets the person receiving the letter.

Type **Subject: Your Application to Music School Records** and press Enter. Notice the light dots between words, which indicate spaces and display when formatting marks are displayed. Also, notice the extra space after each paragraph, and then compare your screen with Figure 5.6.

The subject line is optional, but you should include a subject line in most letters to identify the topic. Depending on your Word settings, a wavy green line may display in the subject line, indicating a potential grammar error.

KEY FEATURE

GO! **Microsoft Procedural Syntax**

All steps are written in Microsoft Procedural Syntax to put the student in the right place at the right time.

Note — Space Between Lines in Your Printed Document

The Cambria font, and many others, uses a slightly larger space between the lines than more traditional fonts like Times New Roman. As you progress in your study of Word, you will use many different fonts and also adjust the spacing between lines.

From the **Office** menu, click **Close**, saving any changes if prompted to do so. Leave Word open for the next project.

Another Way | **To Print a Document**

To Print a document:

• From the Office menu, click Print to display the Print dialog box (to be covered later), from which you can choose a variety of different options, such as printing multiple copies, printing on a different printer, and printing some but not all pages.

• Hold down Ctrl and then press P. This is an alternative to the Office menu command, and opens the Print dialog box.

• Hold down Alt, press F, and then press P. This opens the Print dialog box.

End **You have completed Project 5A**

End-of-Project Icon

All projects in the *GO! Series* have clearly identifiable end points, useful in self-paced or online environments.

Teach (continued)

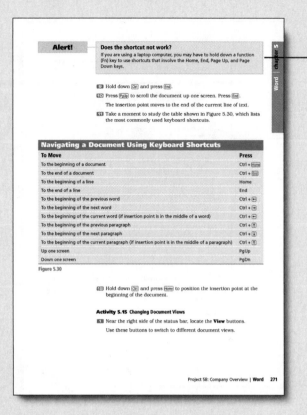

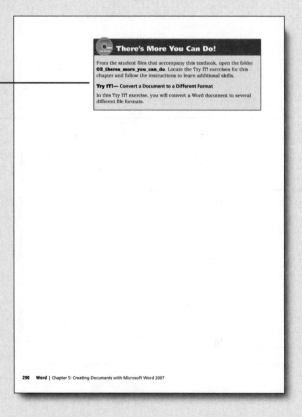

Alert box
Draws students' attention to make sure they aren't getting too far off course.

Another Way box
Shows students other ways of doing tasks.

More Knowledge box
Expands on a topic by going deeper into the material.

Note box
Points out important items to remember.

NEW

There's More You Can Do!
Try IT! exercises that teach students additional skills.

End-of-Chapter Material

Take your pick! Content-based or Outcomes-based projects to choose from. Below is a table outlining the various types of projects that fit into these two categories.

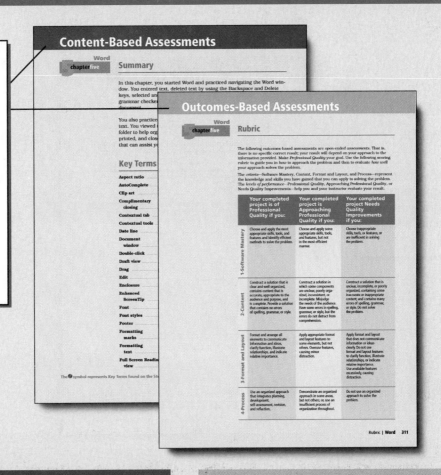

Content-Based Assessments

(Defined solutions with solution files provided for grading)

Project Letter	Name	Objectives Covered
N/A	Summary and Key Terms	
N/A	Multiple Choice	
N/A	Fill-in-the-blank	
C	Skills Review	Covers A Objectives
D	Skills Review	Covers B Objectives
E	Mastering Excel	Covers A Objectives
F	Mastering Excel	Covers B Objectives
G	Mastering Excel	Covers any combination of A and B Objectives
H	Mastering Excel	Covers any combination of A and B Objectives
I	Mastering Excel	Covers all A and B Objectives
J	Business Running Case	Covers all A and B Objectives

Outcomes-Based Assessments

(Open solutions that require a rubric for grading)

Project Letter	Name	Objectives Covered
N/A	Rubric	
K	Problem Solving	Covers as many Objectives from A and B as possible
L	Problem Solving	Covers as many Objectives from A and B as possible.
M	Problem Solving	Covers as many Objectives from A and B as possible.
N	Problem Solving	Covers as many Objectives from A and B as possible.
O	Problem Solving	Covers as many Objectives from A and B as possible.
P	You and GO!	Covers as many Objectives from A and B as possible
Q	GO! Help	Not tied to specific objectives
R	* Group Business Running Case	Covers A and B Objectives

* This project is provided only with the *GO! with Microsoft Office 2007 Introductory* book.

Objectives List

Most projects in the end-of-chapter section begin with a list of the objectives covered.

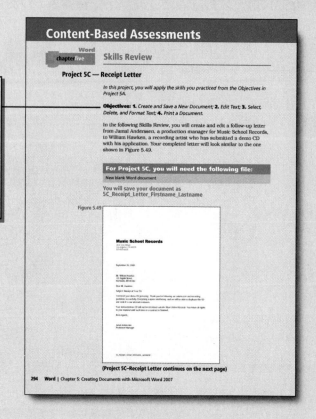

Content-Based Assessments

Word
chapter five   **Skills Review**

Project 5C — Receipt Letter

In this project, you will apply the skills you practiced from the Objectives in Project 5A.

Objectives: 1. Create and Save a New Document; **2.** Edit Text; **3.** Select, Delete, and Format Text; **4.** Print a Document.

In the following Skills Review, you will create and edit a follow-up letter from Jamal Anderssen, a production manager for Music School Records, to William Hawken, a recording artist who has submitted a demo CD with his application. Your completed letter will look similar to the one shown in Figure 5.49.

For Project 5C, you will need the following file:

New blank Word document

You will save your document as
5C_Receipt_Letter_Firstname_Lastname

Figure 5.49

(Project 5C–Receipt Letter continues on the next page)

294   **Word** | Chapter 5: Creating Documents with Microsoft Word 2007

End of Each Project Clearly Marked

Clearly identified end points help separate the end-of-chapter projects.

Content-Based Assessments

Word
chapter five   **Skills Review**

(Project 5C–Receipt Letter continued)

14. Save the changes you have made to your document. Press Ctrl + A to select the entire document. On the **Home tab**, in the **Font group**, click the **Font button arrow**. Scroll as necessary, and watch Live Preview change the document font as you point to different font names. Click to choose **Tahoma**. Recall that you can type *T* in the Font box to move quickly to the fonts beginning with that letter. Click anywhere in the document to cancel the selection.

15. Select the entire first line of text—*Music School Records*. On the Mini toolbar, click the **Font button arrow**, and then click **Arial Black**. With the Mini toolbar still displayed, click the **Font Size button arrow**, and then click **20**. With the Mini toolbar still displayed, click the **Bold** button.

16. Select the second, third, and fourth lines of text, beginning with *2620 Vine Street* and ending with the telephone number. On the Mini toolbar, click the **Font button arrow**, and then click **Arial**. With the Mini toolbar still displayed, click the **Font Size button arrow**, and then click **10**. With the Mini toolbar still displayed, click the **Italic** button.

17. In the paragraph beginning *Your demonstration*, select the text *Music School Records*. On the Mini toolbar, click the **Italic** button, and then click anywhere to deselect the text.

18. Click the **Insert tab**. In the **Header & Footer group**, click the **Footer** button,

and then click **Edit Footer**. On the **Design tab**, in the **Insert group**, click the **Quick Parts** button, and then click **Field**. In the **Field** dialog box, under **Field names**, scroll down and click to choose **FileName**, and then click **OK**. Double-click anywhere in the document to leave the footer area.

19. Click the **Page Layout tab**. In the **Page Setup group**, click the **Margins** button to display the Margins gallery. At the bottom of the **Margins gallery**, click **Custom Margins** to display the **Page Setup** dialog box. Near the top of the **Page Setup** dialog box, click the **Layout tab**. Under **Page**, click the **Vertical alignment arrow**, click **Center**, and then click **OK**.

20. From the **Office** menu, point to the **Print arrow**, and then click **Print Preview** to make a final check of your letter. Follow your instructor's directions for submitting this file. Check your *Chapter Assignment Sheet or Course Syllabus* or consult your instructor to determine if you are to submit your assignments on paper or electronically. To submit electronically, go to Step 22, and then follow the instructions provided by your instructor.

21. On the **Print Preview tab**, in the **Print group**, click the **Print** button. Collect your printout from the printer and submit it as directed.

22. From the **Office** menu, click **Exit Word**, saving any changes if prompted to do so.

End You have completed Project 5C

296   **Word** | Chapter 5: Creating Documents with Microsoft Word 2007

NEW

Rubric

A matrix that states the criteria and standards for grading student work. Used to grade open-ended assessments.

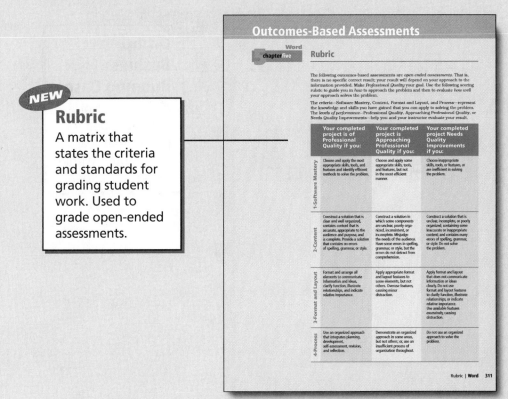

GO! with Help

Students practice using the Help feature of the Office application.

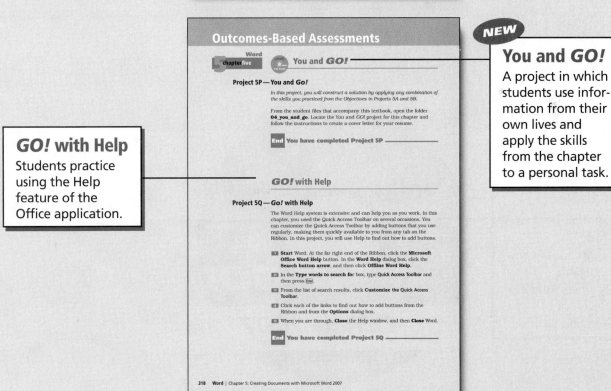

NEW

You and GO!

A project in which students use information from their own lives and apply the skills from the chapter to a personal task.

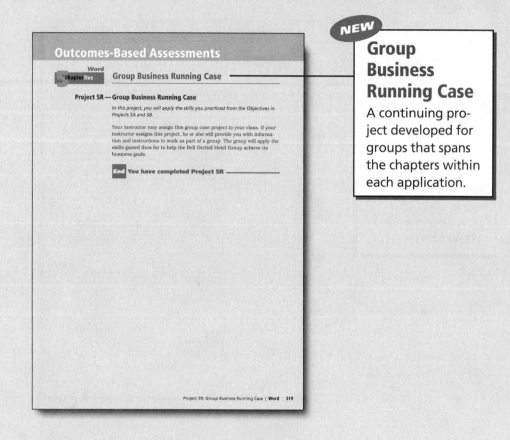

Group Business Running Case

A continuing project developed for groups that spans the chapters within each application.

Student CD includes:

- Student Data Files
- There's More You Can Do!
- Business Running Case
- You and *GO!*

Companion Web site

An interactive Web site to further student leaning.

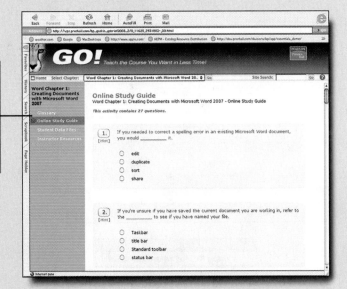

Online Study Guide

Interactive objective-style questions to help students study.

Annotated Instructor Edition

The Annotated Instructor Edition contains a full version of the student textbook that includes tips, supplement references, and pointers on teaching with the *GO!* instructional system.

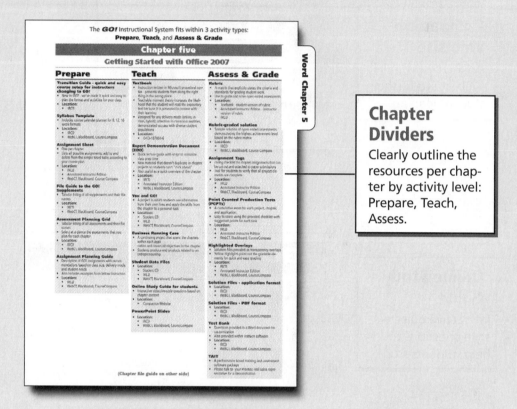

Chapter Dividers

Clearly outline the resources per chapter by activity level: Prepare, Teach, Assess.

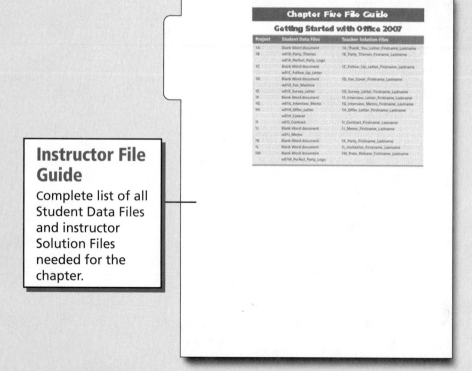

Instructor File Guide

Complete list of all Student Data Files and instructor Solution Files needed for the chapter.

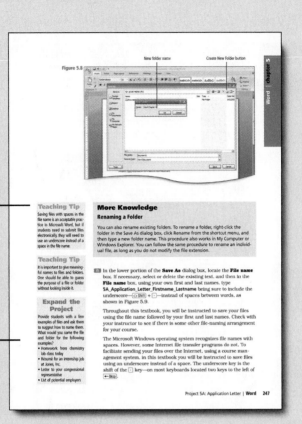

Helpful Hints, Teaching Tips, Expand the Project

References correspond to what is being taught in the student textbook.

NEW

Full-Size Textbook Pages

An instructor copy of the textbook with traditional Instructor Manual content incorporated.

End-of-Chapter Concepts Assessments

Contain the answers for quick reference.

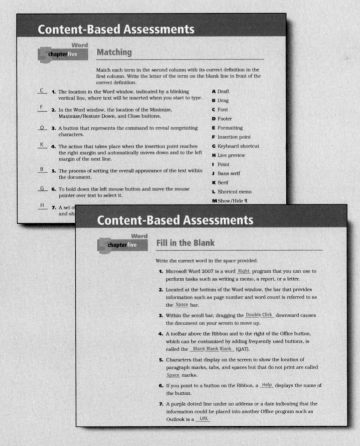

Rubric

A matrix to guide the student on how they will be assessed is reprinted in the Annotated Instructor Edition with suggested weights for each of the criteria and levels of performance. Instructors can modify the weights to suit their needs.

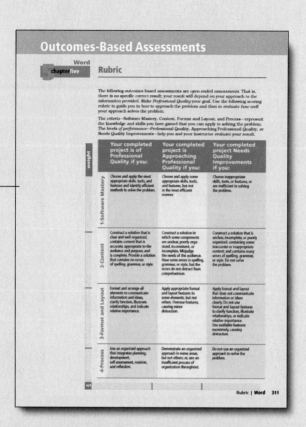

Assignment Tags

NEW

Scoring checklist for assignments. Now also available for Problem-Solving projects.

Highlighted Overlays

Solution files provided as transparency overlays. Yellow highlights point out the gradable elements for quick and easy grading.

GO! with Microsoft® Office 2007

Assignment Tags for GO! with Office 2007
Word Chapter 5

Name:		Project:	5A
Professor:		Course:	
Task	Points	Your Score	
Center text vertically on page	2		
Delete the word "really"	1		
Delete the words "try to"	1		
Replace "last" with "first"	1		
Insert the word "potential"	1		
Replace "John W. Diamond" with "Lucy Burrows"	2		
Change entire document to the Cambria font	2		
Change the first line of text to Arial Black 20 pt. font	2		
Bold the first line of text	2		
Change the 2nd through 4th lines to Arial 10 pt.	2		
Italicize the 2nd through 4th lines of text	2		
Correct/Add footer as instructed	2		
Circled information is incorrect or formatted incorrectly			
Total Points	20	0	

Name:		Project:	5B
Professor:		Course:	
Task	Points	Your Score	
Insert the file w05B_Music_School_Records	4		
Insert the Music Logo	4		
Remove duplicate "and"	2		
Change spelling and grammar errors (4)	8		
Correct/Add footer as instructed	2		
Circled information is incorrect or formatted incorrectly			
Total Points	20	0	

Name:		Project:	5C
Professor:		Course:	
Task	Points	Your Score	
Add four line letterhead	2		
Insert today's date	1		
Add address block, subject line, and greeting	2		
Add two-paragraph body of letter	2		
Add closing, name, and title	2		
In subject line, capitalize "receipt"	1		
Change "standards" to "guidelines"	1		
Insert "quite"	1		
Insert "all"	1		
Change the first line of text to Arial Black 20 pt. font	2		
Bold the first line of text	1		
Change the 2nd through 4th lines to Arial 10 pt.	1		
Italicize the 2nd through 4th lines of text	1		
Correct/add footer as instructed	2		
Circled information is incorrect or formatted incorrectly			
Total Points	20	0	

Name:		Project:	5D
Professor:		Course:	
Task	Points	Your Score	
Insert the file w05D_Marketing	4		
Bold the first two title lines	2		
Correct spelling of "Marketting"	2		
Correct spelling of "geners"	2		
Correct all misspellings of "already"	2		
Correct grammar error "are" to "is"	2		
Insert the Piano image	4		
Correct/add footer as instructed	2		
Circled information is incorrect or formatted incorrectly			
Total Points	20	0	

Music School Records

20 point Arial Black, bold and underline

2620 Vine Street
Los Angeles, CA 90028
323-555-0028

10 point Arial, italic

September 12, 2009

Mr. William Hawken
123 Eighth Street
Harrisville, MI 48740

Text vertically centered on page

Body of document changed to Cambria font, 11 point

Dear William:

Subject: Your Application to Music School Records

Thank you for submitting your application to Music School Records. Our talent scout for Northern Michigan, Catherine McDonald, is very enthusiastic about your music, and the demo CD you submitted certainly confirms her opinion.

Word "really" deleted

We discuss our applications from potential clients during the first week of each month. We will have a decision for you by the second week of October.

Words "try to" deleted

Yours Truly,

Lucy Burroughs

Point-Counted Production Tests (PCPTs)

A cumulative exam for each **project**, **chapter**, and **application**. Easy to score using the provided checklist with suggested points for each task.

GO! with Microsoft® Office 2007 Introductory

Point-Counted Production Test—Project for GO! with Microsoft® Office 2007 Introductory Project 5A

Instructor Name: _____

Course Information: _____

1. Start Word 2007 to begin a new blank document. Save your document as 5A_Cover_Letter_Firstname_Lastname Remember to save your file frequently as you work.

2. If necessary, display the formatting marks. With the insertion point blinking in the upper left corner of the document to the left of the default first paragraph mark, type the current date (you can use AutoComplete).

3. Press Enter three times and type the inside address:

    Music School Records
    2620 Vine Street
    Los Angeles, CA 90028

4. Press Enter three times, and type Dear Ms. Burroughs:

    Press Enter twice, and type Subject: Application to Music School Records

    Press Enter twice, and type the following text (skipping one line between paragraphs):

    I read about Music School Records in Con Brio magazine and I would like to inquire about the possibility of being represented by your company.

    I am very interested in a career in jazz and am planning to relocate to the Los Angeles area in the very near future. I would be interested in learning more about the company and about available opportunities.

    I was a member of my high school jazz band for three years. In addition, I have been playing in the local coffee shop for the last two years. My demo CD, which is enclosed, contains three of my most requested songs.

    I would appreciate the opportunity to speak with you. Thank you for your time and consideration. I look forward to speaking with you about this exciting opportunity.

5. Press Enter three times, and type the closing Sincerely, Press enter four times, and type your name.

6. Insert a footer that contains the file name.

7. Delete the first instance of the word *very* in the second body paragraph, and insert the word modern in front of *jazz*.

Copyright © 2008 Pearson Prentice Hall   Page 1 of 1

Test Bank

Available as TestGen Software or as a Word document for customization.

Chapter 5: Creating Documents with Microsoft Word 2007

Multiple Choice:

1. With word processing programs, how are documents stored?

    A. On a network

    B. On the computer

    C. Electronically

    D. On the floppy disk

Answer: C   **Reference:** Objective 1: Create and Save a New Document   **Difficulty:** Moderate

2. Because you will see the document as it will print, _____ view is the ideal view to use when learning Microsoft Word 2007.

    A. Reading

    B. Normal

    C. Print Layout

    D. Outline

Answer: C   **Reference:** Objective 1: Create and Save a New Document   **Difficulty:** Moderate

3. The blinking vertical line where text or graphics will be inserted is called the:

    A. cursor.

    B. insertion point.

    C. blinking line.

    D. I-beam.

Answer: B   **Reference:** Objective 1: Create and Save a New Document   **Difficulty:** Easy

---

Solution Files–Application and PDF format

 Music School Records

Music School Records discovers, launches, and develops the careers of young artists in classical, jazz, and contemporary music. Our philosophy is to not only shape, distribute, and sell a music product, but to help artists create a career that can last a lifetime. Too often in the music industry, artists are forced to fit their music to a trend that is short-lived. Music School Records does not just follow trends, we take a long-term view of the music industry and help our artists develop a style and repertoire that is fluid and flexible and that will appeal to audiences for years and even decades.

The music industry is constantly changing, but over the last decade, the changes have been enormous. New forms of entertainment such as DVDs, video games, and the Internet mean there is more competition for the leisure dollar in the market. New technologies give consumers more options for buying and listening to music, and they are demanding high quality recordings. Young consumers are comfortable with technology and want the music they love when and where they want it, no matter where they are or what they are doing.

Music School Records embraces new technologies and the sophisticated market of young music lovers. We believe that providing high quality recordings of truly talented artists make for more discerning listeners who will cherish the gift of music for the rest of their lives. The expertise of Music School Records includes:

- Insight into our target market and the ability to reach the desired audience
- The ability to access all current sources of music income
- A management team with years of experience in music commerce
- Innovative business strategies and artist development plans
- Investment in technology infrastructure for high quality recordings and business services

pagexxxix_top.docx

Online Assessment and Training

myitlab is Prentice Hall's new performance-based solution that allows you to easily deliver outcomes-based courses on Microsoft Office 2007, with customized training and defensible assessment. Key features of myitlab include:

A *true* "system" approach: myitlab content is the same as in your textbook.
Project-based *and* skills-based: Students complete real-life assignments.
Advanced reporting *and* gradebook: These include student click stream data.
***No* installation required:** myitlab is completely Web-based. You just need an Internet connection, small plug-in, and Adobe Flash Player.

Ask your Prentice Hall sales representative for a demonstration or visit:

www.prenhall.com/myitlab

chapterone

Getting Started with Outlook 2007

OBJECTIVES

At the end of this chapter you will be able to:

1. Start and Navigate Outlook
2. Read and Respond to E-mail
3. Delete Outlook Information and Close Outlook

OUTCOMES

Mastering these objectives will enable you to:

PROJECT 1A

Read and Respond to E-mail Using Outlook 2007

4. Store Contact Information
5. Manage Tasks
6. Work with the Calendar

PROJECT 1B

Manage Personal Information Using Outlook 2007

Laurel County Community College

Laurel County Community College is located in eastern Pennsylvania and serves urban, suburban, and rural populations. The College offers this diverse area a broad range of academic and vocational programs, including associate degrees, certificate programs, and noncredit continuing education and personal development courses. LCCC makes positive contributions to the community through cultural and athletic programs and partnerships with businesses and nonprofit organizations. The college also provides industry-specific training programs for local businesses through its Economic Development Center.

Getting Started with Microsoft Office Outlook 2007

Do you sometimes find it a challenge to keep up with all the information related to your job, family, and class work? Microsoft Office Outlook 2007 can help. Outlook combines all the features of a *personal information manager* with e-mail capabilities in a program that you can use with other programs within Microsoft Office. One of the most common uses of the personal computer is for e-mail. Outlook's e-mail capabilities make it easy to communicate with coworkers, business contacts, friends, and family members.

As a personal information manager, Outlook enables you to electronically store information about people with whom you communicate, such as their names, addresses, and phone numbers. You can also use Outlook to manage your time. You can record appointments and meetings in a daily schedule, and receive reminders for ones you do not want to forget. You can keep track of tasks you want to complete in a personal to-do list. In this chapter, you will become familiar with Outlook's capabilities as a personal information manager and an e-mail program.

Project 1A **Exploring Outlook 2007**

In Activities 1.1 through 1.9, you will start Microsoft Office Outlook 2007 and become familiar with the parts of Outlook. Then you will handle e-mail and activities for Kesia Toomer, Vice President of Administration and Development at Laurel County Community College. You will read and reply to her e-mail. You will print an e-mail message. Upon completion, your Inbox and e-mail message will look similar to the ones shown in Figure 1.1.

For Project 1A, you will need the following file:

01A_Inbox

You will print
1A_Inbox_Firstname_Lastname
1A_Message_Firstname_Lastname

Figure 1.1
Project 1A—Inbox

Objective 1
Start and Navigate Outlook

Microsoft Office Outlook 2007 has two functions: It is an e-mail program and it is a personal information manager. Among other things, a *personal information manager* enables you to electronically store information about your friends, family members, coworkers, customers, suppliers, or other individuals with whom you communicate. You can also use a personal information manager to keep track of your daily schedule, tasks you need to complete, and other personal and business-related information. Thus, Outlook's major parts include Mail for e-mail and Calendar, Contacts, and Tasks for personal information management.

Your e-mail and personal information in Outlook is stored in folders, and there are separate folders for each of Outlook's components. For example, one of the folders in the Mail component is called the *Inbox*. Outlook presents information in *views*, which are ways to look at similar information in different formats and arrangements. Mail, Contacts, Calendar, and Tasks all have different views.

Alert!

Complete This Project in One Working Session

Because Outlook stores information on the hard drive of the system at which you are working, it is recommended that you schedule enough time to complete this project in one working session, unless you are working on a system that is used only by you. Allow approximately one to two hours for Project 1A.

Activity 1.1 Starting Outlook

Start Outlook in the same manner as you start other Microsoft Office 2007 programs.

1 On the Windows taskbar, click the **Start** button start .

2 From the displayed **Start** menu, locate the Outlook program, and then click **Microsoft Office Outlook**. If necessary, on the Outlook title bar, click the Maximize button 🔲 to maximize the Outlook window.

Organizations and individuals store computer programs in a variety of ways. The Outlook program might be located under All Programs or Microsoft Office or at the top of the Start menu. Compare your screen with Figure 1.2 for an example.

Figure 1.2

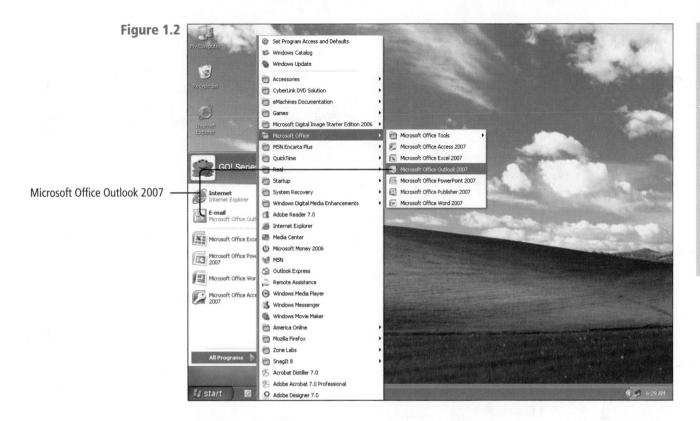

Microsoft Office Outlook 2007 ——

3 Look at the opening Outlook screen, and take a moment to study the main parts of the screen, as shown in Figure 1.3 and as described in the table in Figure 1.4.

The default view when you open Outlook is *Outlook Today*, which is a summary view of your schedule, tasks, and e-mail for the current day.

Alert!

Does your Outlook screen differ from the one shown in Figure 1.3?

Your program window might display the Inbox instead of Outlook Today. The starting appearance of the screen depends on the settings that were established when Outlook was installed on the computer you are using. If your Outlook data is stored in a personal folders file, it will likely be named *Personal Folders*. If your data is stored on a Microsoft Exchange Server, it will be named *Mailbox*. To see Outlook Today, click either Personal Folders or Mailbox.

If Outlook asks you to logon or choose a profile, follow your instructor's directions for starting Outlook. If the Outlook 2007 Startup Wizard appears, click Next, select No, and click Next. Click the Continue with no e-mail support check box, and then click Finish.

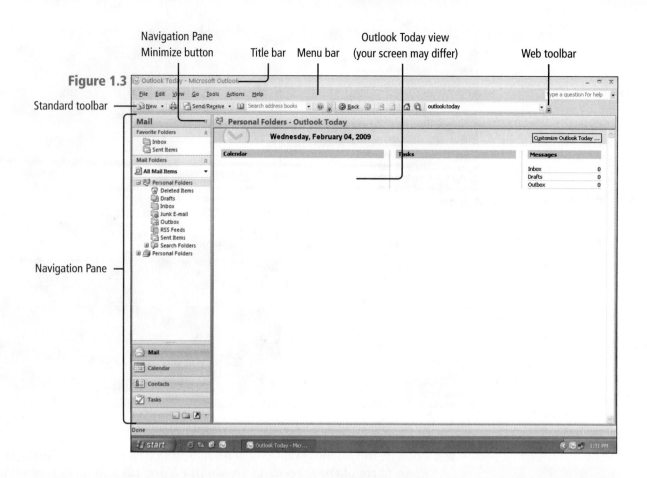

Figure 1.3

Navigation Pane Minimize button · Title bar · Menu bar · Outlook Today view (your screen may differ) · Web toolbar · Standard toolbar · Navigation Pane

Microsoft Outlook Screen Elements

Screen Element	Description
Title bar	Displays the program name and the name of the window. The Minimize, Maximize/Restore Down, and Close buttons display on the right side of the title bar.
Menu bar	Contains lists of commands grouped by category. To display a menu, click the menu name.
Standard toolbar	Contains buttons for the most commonly used commands in Outlook. Which buttons display will depend on Outlook's current view.
Web toolbar	Contains buttons that allow the Outlook Today pane to function as a Web browser.
Navigation Pane	A group of smaller panes containing shortcuts to Outlook's components. The top part typically shows folders and the lower portion contains buttons to Outlook's major tools.
Outlook Today	A summary view of your schedule, tasks, and e-mail for the current day.

Figure 1.4

Activity 1.2 Exploring Outlook Using the Navigation Pane and Folder List

A convenient way to move among—navigate—Outlook's different components is to use the Navigation Pane, which is located on the left side of the Outlook window. The ***Navigation Pane*** provides quick access to Outlook's components. Outlook uses folders to organize information, and you can also use the Folder List to move around Outlook. Individual folders store ***items***. An item is an element of information in Outlook, such as a message, a contact name, a task, or an appointment. As you manage the activities of Kesia Toomer, the Navigation Pane and Folder List will be your tools for moving around Outlook.

1 Be sure that your **Navigation Pane** is displayed as shown in Figure 1.3. If necessary, on the menu bar, click **View**, point to **Navigation Pane**, and click **Normal** to display it.

The Navigation Pane displays as a column on the left side of the Outlook window. The upper portion of the Navigation Pane contains smaller panes. The lower portion contains buttons to quickly display frequently used folders.

2 If necessary, in the **Navigation Pane**, click the **Mail** button ⬜ Mail . In the upper portion of the **Navigation Pane**, under **Mail Folders**, click **Inbox**.

The Inbox folder displays. The middle pane of the Outlook window lists any e-mail messages you have received. On the right side of the screen is the ***Reading Pane***, a window in which you can preview an e-mail message without actually opening it. If you have messages, the currently selected message displays in the Reading Pane. On the far right of the screen is the ***To-Do Bar*** which provides quick access to daily tasks.

Alert!

Does your screen differ?

Depending on the configuration of Outlook on your system, your Reading Pane and To-Do Bar may not display. To show the Reading Pane, from the View menu, point to Reading Pane and click Right. To show the To-Do Bar, from the View menu, point to To-Do Bar and click Minimized.

3 In the **Navigation Pane** on the far left of the screen, click the **Minimize the Navigation Pane** button ⬜ « .

The most used features of the Navigation Pane display as buttons along the left side of the screen.

4 In the **Navigation Pane**, click the **Expand the Navigation Pane** button ⬜ » .

The Navigation Pane returns to its normal view and the Expand button changes back to the Minimize button. Most panes in Outlook can be maximized and minimized in this way.

5 In the **Navigation Pane**, click the **Calendar** button ⬜ Calendar to display the Calendar folder.

The right portion of the Outlook window displays the calendar for the current day, and the upper two panes of the Navigation Pane display calendar-related information. At the bottom of the screen, the Tasks pane will display task items. The Web toolbar is no longer displayed, and the Standard toolbar changes the commands that are available. In this manner, each of Outlook's folder views displays different information.

6 In the **Navigation Pane**, click the **Contacts** button ⬛ Contacts to display the Contacts folder. If necessary, in the Navigation Pane, under Current View, click the Simple List radio button.

The Contacts folder functions as an address book. If no contacts have been created, the Contacts pane will be blank. The Standard toolbar shows buttons related to managing contacts and the To-Do Bar is available at the right of the screen.

7 In the **Navigation Pane**, click the **Tasks** button ⬛ Tasks to display the Tasks folder.

By default, the Pane displays tasks arranged by Due Date. If no tasks have been created, this list is blank.

8 In the **Navigation Pane**, under **My Tasks**, click **Tasks** ⬛ Tasks .

The Tasks list provides another way to view any pending tasks.

9 In the lower portion of the **Navigation Pane**, locate the four small buttons that display an *icon*—a graphic representation of an object that you can click to open that object. Point to each one to display its *ScreenTip*, which is a small box that displays the name of a screen element, and then click the **Folder List** button ⬛ to display the Folder List in the upper portion of the **Navigation Pane**, as shown in Figure 1.5.

The right portion of the Outlook window continues to display the Tasks folder; the upper portion of the Navigation Pane displays the Folder List. Folders shown in the Navigation Pane may contain more folders than can fit in the All Folders pane. *Scrolling* is the action of moving a pane or window vertically (up or down) or horizontally (side to side) to bring unseen areas into view. Click the scroll arrow or drag the scroll box to move the pane.

Figure 1.5

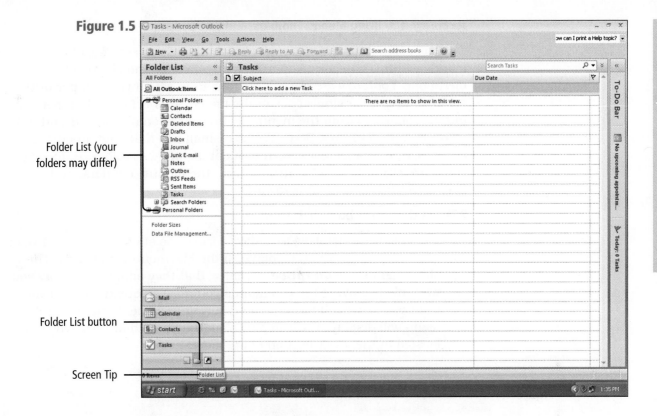

Folder List (your folders may differ)

Folder List button

Screen Tip

10 In the upper portion of the **Navigation Pane**, under **All Folders**, locate the first folder, which is also called the *root folder*—the folder on a drive from which all other folders branch. Click either **Personal Folders** or **Mailbox**.

The Outlook Today view displays.

11 Below **All Folders**, click **Inbox** to display the Inbox folder.

12 In the **Navigation Pane**, click the **Mail** button to display just the Mail folders.

Outlook hides the Folder List when you click a button in the Navigation Pane.

Activity 1.3 Using Menus, Toolbars, and ScreenTips

Outlook commands are organized in *menus*, which are lists of commands within a category. You access menu commands by using the menu bar. *Toolbars* are rows of buttons from which you can perform commands using a single click of the mouse; this is faster than performing the command from the menu. Toolbars are usually located under the menu bar. Recall that a ScreenTip is a small box that contains the name or a descriptive label of a screen element, such as a toolbar button. As you move around Kesia Toomer's Inbox, the menus, toolbars, and ScreenTips will be available to you.

1 On the menu bar, click **File**.

The File menu displays in a short format, as shown in Figure 1.6, or in a full format, which displays all the File menu commands. The short menus are *adaptive*, meaning that they adapt to the way you work by displaying the commands you most frequently use. If you want to see the full format, you can wait a moment, and the full menu will display. You can also click the Expand arrows, which are located in the lower portion of the menu.

Figure 1.6

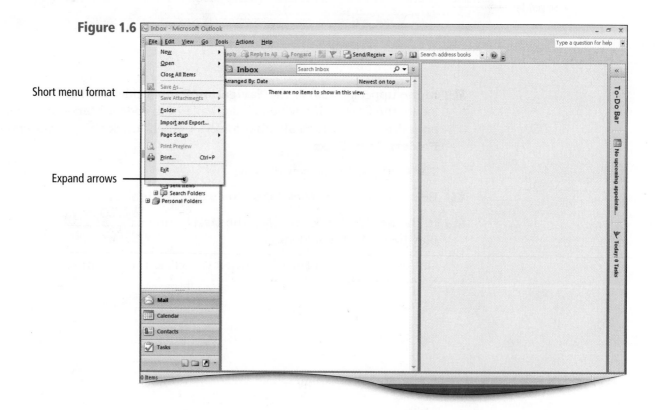

Short menu format

Expand arrows

2 From the displayed **File** menu, point to, but do not click, the **New** command to display the submenu, as shown in Figure 1.7.

When you point to a command on the menu, the command is shaded and surrounded by a border. Commands that have triangles next to their names will display a *submenu*, which is another menu of commands.

Ellipsis (…) indicates that the command
will display a dialog box or task pane

Submenu

Figure 1.7

Gray lettering indicates
that the command is
currently unavailable

Triangle indicates that a
submenu will display

Toolbar button for
Print command

Keyboard shortcut for
Print command

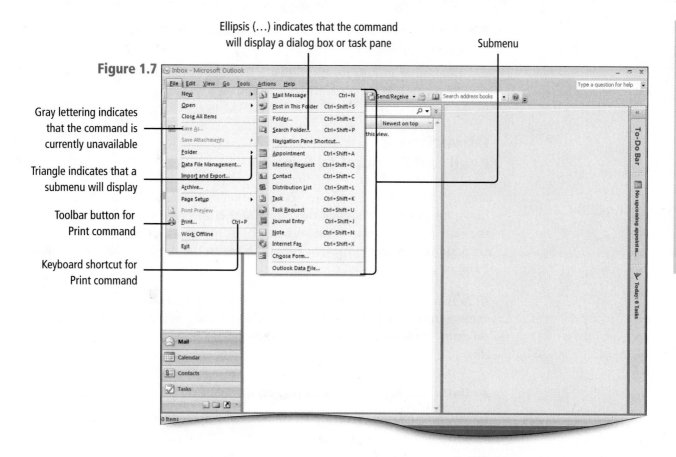

3 Without clicking, move the pointer down the list of commands on the **File** menu.

Commands that are shaded or gray indicate that the command is currently unavailable. Commands that display an ellipsis (. . .) after the name will open a dialog box or a task pane.

4 Look to the right of the **Print** command and notice the keyboard shortcut, *Ctrl+P*.

A **keyboard shortcut** is a combination of keys on the keyboard that perform a command. Many Outlook commands can be accomplished in more than one way. To use the keyboard shortcut for the Print command, press and hold down Ctrl and then press P. The result is the same as clicking File on the menu bar and then clicking Print on the File menu.

5 To the left of the **Print** command, notice the image of the toolbar button that represents the Print command on the toolbar, as shown in Figure 1.7.

6 Move the pointer away from the menu, and click anywhere in the Outlook window to close the menu without executing any commands.

7 On the Standard toolbar, point to the **New** button 📄 New.

When you position the pointer over a button, Outlook highlights the button and displays a ScreenTip, which describes the button as *New Mail Message*.

8 Point to each button on the Standard toolbar, observing the ScreenTip for each button.

Shaded or gray buttons indicate that the command represented by the button is not currently available.

Objective 2
Read and Respond to E-mail

Messages you receive are stored in Outlook's Inbox folder. Each message has a header that displays the name of the message sender, the subject, the date and time sent, and sometimes other information. You can respond to a received message by replying to the message in the Reading Pane or by opening the message.

In Activities 1.4 through 1.7, you will work with messages that you will import into your Inbox. This will enable you to work with and respond to different types of received messages.

Activity 1.4 Importing Messages into the Inbox

In this activity, you will import Kesia Toomer's received messages into your Inbox.

1 Locate and insert the CD that came with this textbook. From the **Start** menu, click **My Computer**, create a file folder named **Outlook** for your Outlook files on the storage location that you will be using for your projects in this chapter—for example, on your USB flash drive, your floppy disk, your hard drive, or a network drive that has been assigned to you.

2 From **My Computer**, navigate to the CD and display its file list, open the **01_student_data_files** folder, and then right-click the **chapter_01_outlook** folder. From the displayed shortcut menu, click **Copy**.

Right-click is the action of clicking an object with the right mouse button; a *shortcut menu* is a list of context-related commands that displays when you right-click a screen element.

3 From **My Computer**, navigate to the location where you are storing files for this project, for example, your USB drive. From the **Edit** menu, click **Paste**. Your files are ready to use for the Outlook projects in this chapter.

4 **Close** My Computer and return to the **Outlook** window. In the **Navigation Pane**, under **Favorite Folders**, click **Inbox** to make the Inbox folder the current folder.

5 From the **File** menu, click **Import and Export**.

The Import and Export Wizard dialog box displays. A *wizard* is a tool that walks you step-by-step through a process.

6 In the **Import and Export Wizard** dialog box, under **Choose an action to perform**, make sure that **Import from another program or file** is selected, and then click **Next**.

7 In the **Import a File** dialog box, under **Select file type to import from**, click the **down scroll arrow** until the lower portion of the list displays.

8 Click **Personal Folder File (.pst)**, and then click **Next**. In the displayed **Import Personal Folders** dialog box, click **Browse**.

9 In the displayed **Open Personal Folders** dialog box, click the **Look in arrow** at the right edge of the **Look in** box to view a list of the drives and folders available on your system. See Figure 1.8 as an example—the drives and folders displayed on your screen will differ.

Look in box　　List of available drives and folders (yours will differ)　　Look in arrow

Figure 1.8

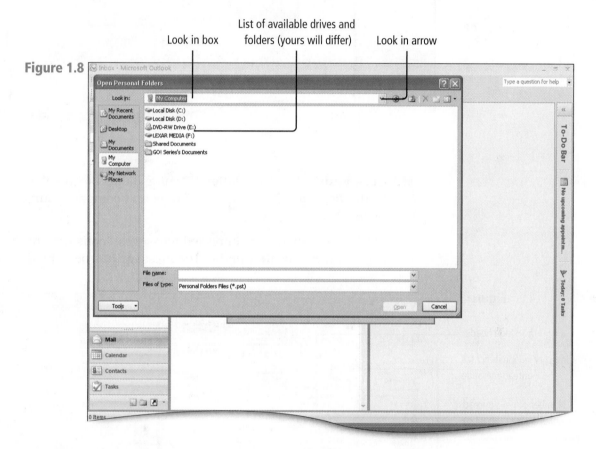

10 Navigate to the drive and folder to which you copied the Outlook files in Steps 1 through 3. Locate **01A_Inbox**, and click one time to select it. Then, in the lower right corner of the **Open Personal Folders** dialog box, click **Open**.

The Open Personal Folders dialog box closes, and the path and file name display in the File to import box. Under Options, Replace duplicates with items imported is already selected.

11 Click **Next**, and then compare your screen with Figure 1.9.

The Import Personal Folders dialog box displays the folder structure for the file you are going to import.

Figure 1.9

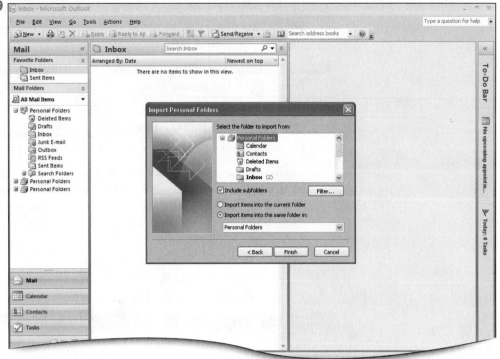

12 Click **Finish**. If a Translation Warning dialog box displays, click OK. Under **Personal Folders**, click **Inbox** and compare your screen with Figure 1.10.

The Inbox displays the imported messages. Icons next to the message sender indicate whether the message has been read or not.

Figure 1.10

Message header

Closed envelope indicates unread message

Number of new, unread messages in the Inbox

Open envelope indicates read message

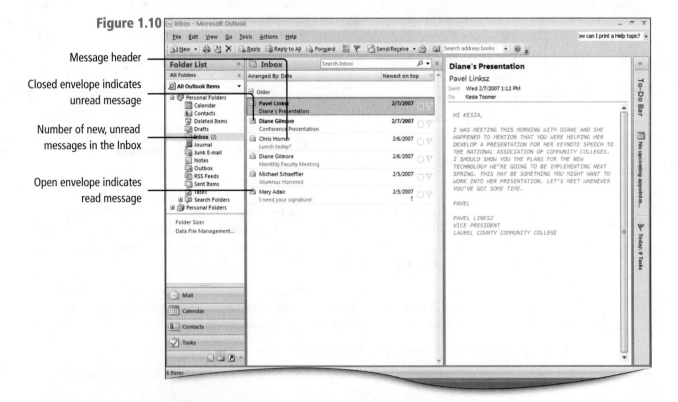

Alert!

Does your screen differ?

Your Outlook screen may differ slightly from the one shown. In Figure 1.10, above the first message, *Beyond Next Month* is indicated. The label above your first messages may vary depending on the date of your computer's system clock.

Activity 1.5 Opening, Navigating, and Closing an E-mail Message

You can read messages in two ways. You can read the text of shorter messages in the Reading Pane without opening the message. When the Reading Pane is not displayed or the text of the message is too long to fit in the Reading Pane, you can open the message. When you open a message, it is displayed in an Outlook *form*, which is a window for displaying and collecting information. There are forms for messages, contacts, tasks, and appointments. In this activity, you will view Kesia Toomer's messages in several ways.

1 Look at the **Inbox**, and take a moment to study the messages shown in Figure 1.10.

In the Navigation Pane, the number in parentheses found to the right of Inbox displays the number of unread messages. The Inbox Pane lists the message header for each message. **Message headers** include basic information about an e-mail message such as the sender's name, the date sent, and the subject. The message header for an e-mail that has not yet been read or opened is displayed in bold, and the icon at the left shows a closed envelope. After a message has been read, the bold is removed and the icon changes to an open envelope.

2 Locate the second message in the **Inbox**, which is from *Diane Gilmore* and has as its subject *Conference Presentation*. Click the message header one time to display the message in the Reading Pane.

The *Conference Presentation* message is too long to display entirely in the Reading Pane; however, you can scroll down to view the remainder of the message. Or you may prefer to open the message to read it.

3 In the **Inbox Pane**, note that the message header from *Pavel Linksz* is no longer bold and displays an open envelope icon.

In response to Book's note, Pavel's message will be selected by default when the Inbox is imported. It is therefore marked as read as soon as you click any other message.

4 In the **Inbox Pane**, double-click the **Conference Presentation** message header to open it in its own window. Alternatively, right-click the message, and click Open. Compare your screen with Figure 1.11.

A separate window opens and displays the message, which is the Message form. The area above the text of the message contains the message header information, which includes the sender's name and the date of the message.

Figure 1.11

Message header information —

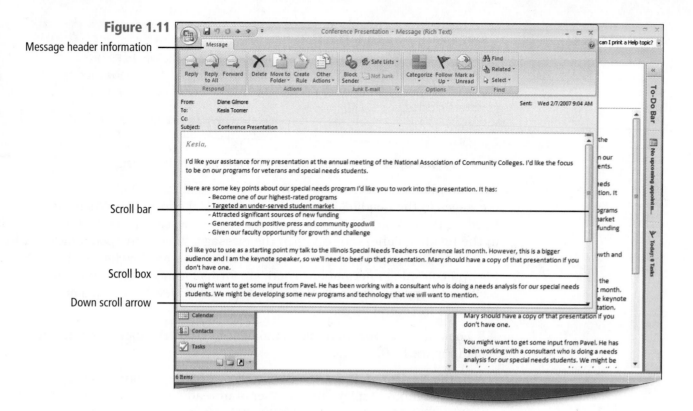

Scroll bar —

Scroll box —

Down scroll arrow —

5 In the vertical scroll bar of the Message form, click the **down scroll arrow** or drag the scroll box down until the lower portion of the message displays.

6 Hold down Ctrl and press Home to scroll to the beginning of the message.

You can use a number of different keystrokes to move within the message, as described in the table in Figure 1.12.

Keystrokes for Moving within a Message	Result
Ctrl + End	Moves to the end of the message
Ctrl + Home	Moves to the beginning of the message
Page Up	Moves up one window
PageDown	Moves down one window
↑	Moves up one line
↓	Moves down one line

Figure 1.12

7 Click the **Close** button ☒ to close the Message form.

8 Locate the third message in the Inbox, which is the message from *Chris Horner* with the subject heading *Lunch Today?*, and then open it by double-clicking.

9 **Close** ☒ the Message form, and then view the remaining Inbox messages in the Reading Pane.

Activity 1.6 Configuring Outlook and Replying to a Message

If your computer is connected and *online*—connected to your organization's network or to the public Internet—Outlook's default setting is to send messages immediately when the Send button in the Message form is clicked. Copies of sent messages are then stored in the Sent Items folder. If you are *offline*, not connected to a network or to the public Internet, messages are stored in the Outbox. In this activity, you will configure an e-mail account for Kesia Toomer and then configure Outlook to store all your sent messages in the Outbox instead of actually sending the messages. An *e-mail account* provides a user with a unique address that he or she can use to receive and send e-mail. You will then reply to one of Kesia Toomer's Inbox messages.

1 From the **Tools** menu, open the **Account Settings** dialog box. In the **Account Settings** dialog box, make sure that **E-mail** is the active tab and click the **New** button New... .

2 In the **Add New E-mail Account** dialog box, click **Next**. Select the **Manually configure server settings** option and click **Next** two times. In the **Your Name** box, type **Kesia Toomer** and in the **E-mail Address box**, type **KToomer@LaurelCCC.edu** Set the **Account Type** to **POP3**, the **Incoming mail server** to **mail.LaurelCCC.edu** and the **Outgoing mail server** to **SMTP.LaurelCCC.edu** Accept KToomer as the user name and set the **Password** to **12345** Compare your screen with Figure 1.13, and then click **Next**. Click **Finish**, and then click **Close**.

Outlook is configured to send and receive e-mail for Kesia Toomer. When configuring Outlook to handle your own e-mail, your Internet service provider (ISP) or Network Administrator will provide your e-mail address, account type, mail server names, user name, and password.

Figure 1.13

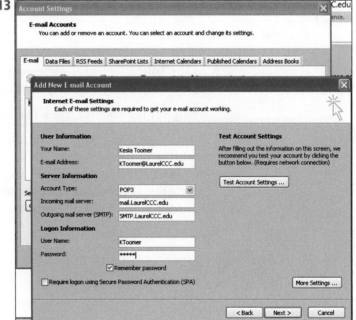

From the **Tools** menu, click **Options**. In the **Options** dialog box, click the **Mail Setup tab**. Under **Send/Receive**, clear the **Send immediately when connected** check box, if necessary.

In the **Options** dialog box, click the **Send/Receive** button
Send/Receive... . In the **Send/Receive Groups** dialog box, under **Setting for group "All Accounts,"** clear all five check boxes if necessary. Compare your dialog box with Figure 1.14. Click **Close**, and then click **OK**.

Outlook is configured to store all sent messages in the Outbox.

Figure 1.14

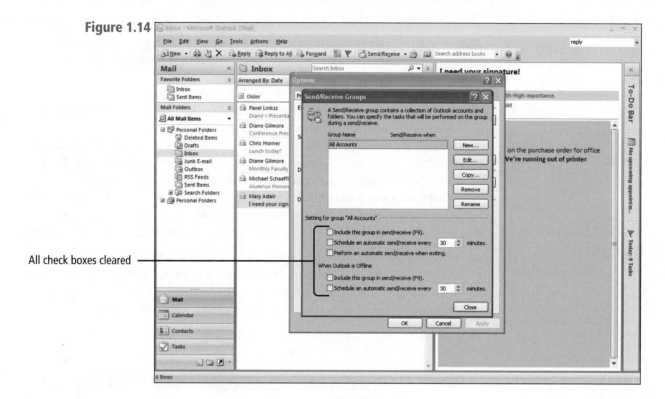

All check boxes cleared

In the **Inbox**, select the message from *Diane Gilmore* that has the subject **Monthly Faculty Meeting** to display it in the Reading Pane. Then, on the toolbar, click the **Reply** button Reply.

A Message form displays. Outlook adds the prefix *RE:* to the subject and title of the message. **RE** is commonly used to mean *in regard to* or *regarding*. The text of the original message is included in the message area of the form, and Outlook places the sender's e-mail address in the To box. Compare your screen with Figure 1.15.

Figure 1.15

Sender's e-mail address
automatically placed in the To box

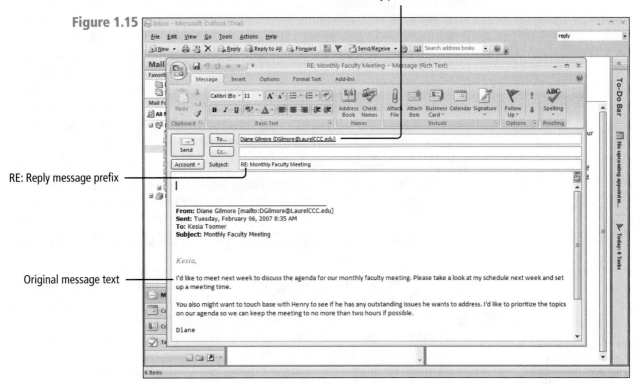

RE: Reply message prefix ————

Original message text ————

6 With the insertion point at the top of the message area, type **Diane**, and press Enter two times. Type **I have scheduled the faculty meeting for next Wednesday at 2 P.M.** Press Enter two times, and type **Kesia**

A message reply is typed above the original message so that the recipient does not have to scroll down to see your reply. Note that you can click the Maximize button on the Message form title bar if you want to see more of the message as you type.

7 Click the **Send** button.

The message is sent to the Outbox, and the Message form closes.

More Knowledge

Servers and Microsoft Exchange Server Accounts

Your e-mail account may require a Microsoft Exchange Server account. A *Microsoft Exchange Server* is an e-mail-based communications server for businesses and organizations. A *server* is a computer or device on a network that handles shared network resources. Microsoft Exchanger Server functions as a mail server for a business or organization. A few Outlook features require a Microsoft Exchange Server e-mail account. If your e-mail account requires Microsoft Exchange Server, contact your organization's network administrator or help desk for assistance. Home users typically do not have Microsoft Exchange Server accounts. Most home users have a POP3 e-mail account with an Internet service provider. ISPs provide their users with specific account information.

Activity 1.7 Printing the Inbox and a Message

Recall that Outlook organizes its information in folders. To print information in Outlook, each folder type has one or more predefined print styles associated with it. A ***print style*** is a combination of paper and page settings that determines the way items print. For the Inbox folder, there are two predefined print styles—Table Style and Memo Style. The ***Table Style*** lists the contents of a folder on a single page and provides limited information about each item. The ***Memo Style*** prints a single item on a single page and provides detailed information about that item. In this activity, you will print Kesia's Inbox and one of her sent messages.

1 Be sure your **Inbox** folder is displayed. From the **File** menu, point to **Page Setup**, and then click **Table Style**. In the displayed **Page Setup: Table Style** dialog box, click the **Format tab**, and then notice the **Preview** image of what your printed document will look like.

Use Table Style to print multiple items in a folder, such as the contents of the Inbox.

2 In the **Page Setup: Table Style** dialog box, click the **Header/Footer tab.** Under **Footer,** in the first white box delete any existing text. Using your own first and last names, type **1A_Inbox_Firstname_Lastname** Do not be concerned if your text wraps to another line. In the center and right footer boxes, delete any existing information. Under **Header**, delete any existing text in the three boxes. Compare your screen with Figure 1.16.

Headers and footers may include the user name, the page number, the number of pages, and the print date and time, or they may include other information. Although the text you type in the Footer box may wrap to two lines, when the page is printed, the footer usually displays on a single line.

Figure 1.16

Footer information ——

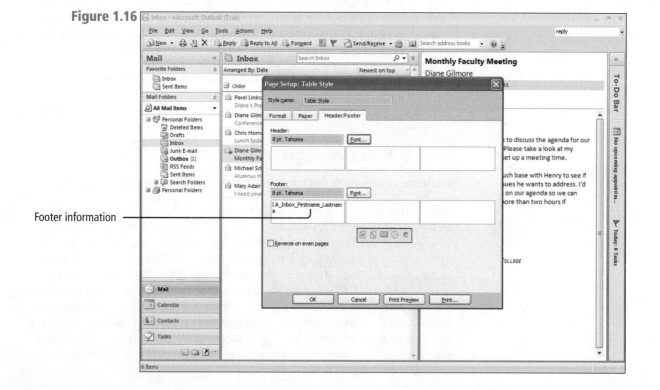

Alert!

Does your screen show a different header or footer?

Outlook remembers previously entered headers and footers. The boxes for this information in the Page Setup dialog box may indicate a previous user's name or some other information. You can enter new information in these boxes and Outlook will retain this information for the next header or footer you print in this print style.

3 At the bottom of the **Page Setup: Table Style** dialog box, click **Print Preview**.

The Inbox list displays as it will appear when printed. The pointer displays as a magnifying glass with a plus sign in it, indicating that you can magnify the view.

4 Point to the lower portion of the document, and click one time to enlarge the lower portion of the preview.

The lower portion of the document is enlarged and easier to read. The pointer changes to a magnifying glass with a minus sign in it.

5 Click one time anywhere in the document to return the view to its previous magnification. On the Print Preview toolbar, click the **Print** button ⊟ Print... , and then compare your screen with Figure 1.17.

The print preview closes, and the Print dialog box displays. In the Print dialog box, you can specify the rows of the Inbox to print, the number of copies to print, and the printer to use. The printer that displays will be the printer that is configured for your computer.

Number of copies

Figure 1.17

Selected Printer (yours will be different)

Memo Style

Rows of the Inbox to print

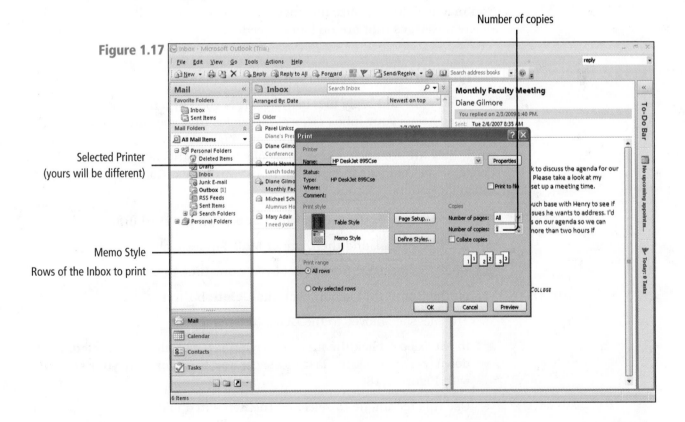

6 In the **Print** dialog box, click **OK**.

From the printer connected to your system, collect your copy of the Inbox list.

7 In the **Navigation Pane**, under **Mail Folders**, click **Outbox** to display the Outbox folder. Click the **RE: Monthly Faculty Meeting** message in the Outbox one time to select it.

8 From the **File** menu, click **Print**.

The Print dialog box displays. When you select an individual message to print, Outlook uses the Memo Style by default; thus, *Memo Style* is already selected. Memo Style prints the text of the selected items one at a time. Use Memo Style to print individual items, such as an entire e-mail message.

9 Click **Page Setup**. In the **Page Setup: Memo Style** dialog box, click the **Header/Footer tab.** Under **Footer,** delete any existing information in the three boxes. In the left **Footer** box, using your own name, type **1A_Message_Firstname_Lastname** Delete any information in the three **Header** boxes and click **OK**.

10 In the **Print** dialog box, click **OK** to print the message.

Objective 3
Delete Outlook Information and Close Outlook

After you have started receiving a large number of e-mail messages, you will need to manage the contents of your Inbox and other mail folders. You may need to organize messages into folders. You will also need to delete messages that are no longer needed.

Activity 1.8 Deleting Outlook Messages

After you read and reply to a message, it is good practice to delete it. Doing so keeps your Inbox clear of messages that you have already handled. It is also a good idea to delete contacts, tasks, and calendar items when they are completed or become obsolete. In this activity, you will delete Kesia Toomer's information from your Inbox, Contacts, Tasks, and Calendar folders.

1 If necessary, in the **Navigation Pane**, click the **Mail** button [Mail], and then, under **Mail Folders**, click **Inbox**.

2 Click the message from *Pavel Linksz* one time to select it, and then, on the Standard toolbar, click the **Delete** button [X].

The message moves to the Deleted Items folder.

3 In the **Inbox**, click the first message if it is not already selected, hold down [⇧ Shift], click the last message, and then compare your screen with Figure 1.18.

Use this technique to select all the items in a folder.

Figure 1.18

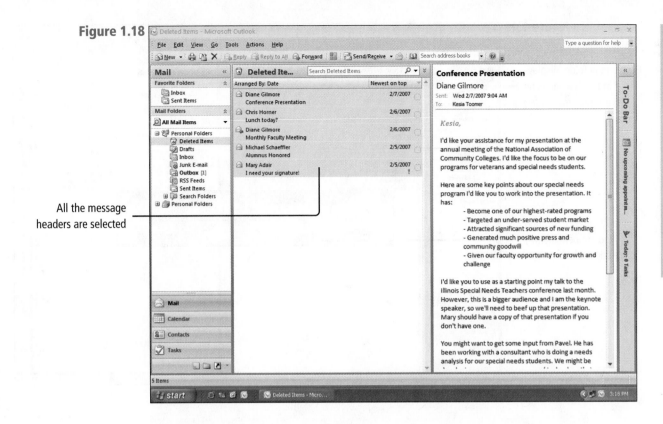

All the message headers are selected

4 On the menu bar, display the **Edit** menu, and notice the **Delete** command. To the left of the command is a reminder that this command can be performed using one click on the toolbar. To the right of the command is a reminder that a keyboard shortcut is available for the command. From the displayed menu, click **Delete**.

The selected messages are deleted, and the Inbox is empty.

5 In the **Navigation Pane**, under **Mail Folders**, click the **Outbox** folder. Delete the contents of this folder.

6 Click the **Contacts** button [Contacts]. While holding [Ctrl], press [A] From the Standard toolbar, click **Delete** [X].

7 Click the **Folder List** button [📁]. Under **Personal Folders**, click the **Deleted Items** folder.

8 Right click the **Deleted Items** folder and from the shortcut menu, click **Empty "Deleted Items" Folders**. Compare your screen with Figure 1.19.

Outlook displays a warning box indicating that you are permanently deleting the selected items.

Figure 1.19

First item in folder displays in the Reading Pane (your screen may differ)

All the items in the folder are selected

Warning box indicating you are permanently deleting selected items

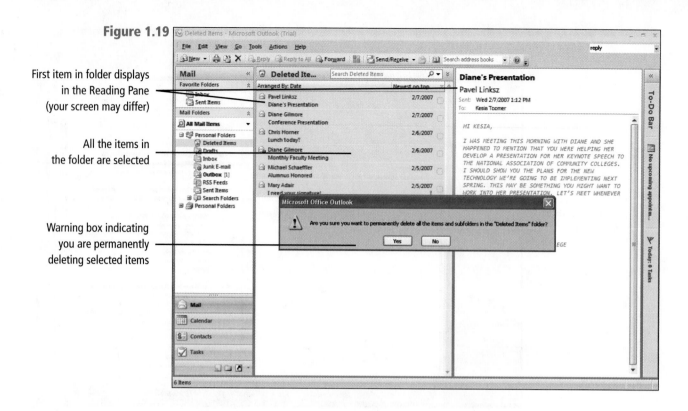

9 In the **Microsoft Office Outlook** dialog box, click **Yes** to permanently delete the items and empty the folder.

Activity 1.9 Resetting Outlook Defaults and Closing Outlook

In this activity, you will delete the e-mail account for Kesia Toomer, restore Outlook's default settings, and close Outlook. You should always leave Outlook with its default settings for the next student or class.

1 From the **Tools** menu, display the **Options** dialog box, and then click the **Mail Setup tab**. Under **Send/Receive**, select the **Send immediately when connected** check box. Then, to the right of the check box, click the **Send/Receive** button [Send/Receive...].

2 In the **Send/Receive Groups** dialog box, under **Setting for group "All Accounts"**, select both the **Include this group in send/receive (F9)** check boxes. Under **Setting for group "All Accounts"**, click the **Schedule an automatic send/receive** check box (if this is a default setting on your computer). Click **Close**, and then click **OK**.

Outlook's default settings for sending and receiving messages are restored.

3 From the **Tools** menu, open the **Account Settings** dialog box. Select the account you created for *KToomer* and click **Remove** [✕ Remove]. Outlook asks if you want to delete the account. Click **Yes**, and then **Close** the dialog box.

4 From the **File** menu, point to **Page Setup**, and then click **Define Print Styles**. Compare your screen with Figure 1.20.

Figure 1.20

Define Print Styles dialog box —

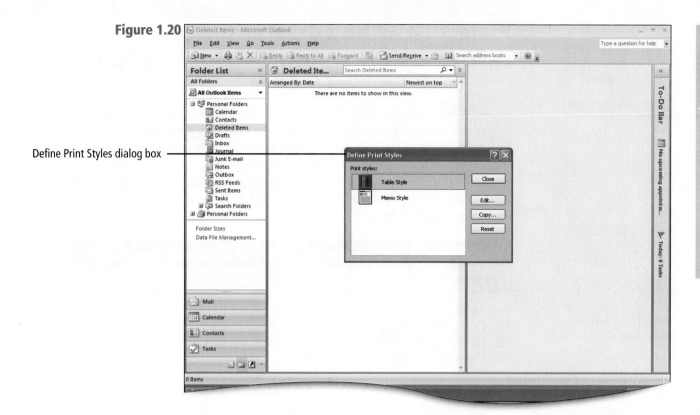

 In the **Define Print Styles** dialog box, with **Table Style** selected, click the **Reset** button and then click **OK**. Click to select the **Memo Style**. Click **Reset**, and then click **OK**. In the **Define Print Styles** dialog box, click **Close**.

The headers and footers in the Table Style and Memo Style print styles that you modified in previous activities are restored to their default settings. Resetting the Table Style in this folder also resets the Table Style you used in the Tasks folder.

 From the **File** menu, click **Exit** to close Outlook. Alternatively, click the **Close** button.

End **You have completed Project 1A** ─────────

Project 1B **Manage Personal Information Using Outlook 2007**

In Activities 1.10 through 1.15, you will handle activities for Kesia Toomer, Vice President of Administration and Development at Laurel County Community College. You will store contact and task information, and record appointments in a daily schedule. You will print the Contacts and To-Do list, and a schedule for the day. Upon completion, your Contacts list, To-Do list, and Calendar will look similar to the ones shown in Figure 1.21.

For Project 1B, you will need the following file:

01B_Personal_Folders

You will print
1B_Contacts_Firstname_Lastname
1B_To-Do_List_Firstname_Lastname
1B_Calendar_Firstname_Lastname

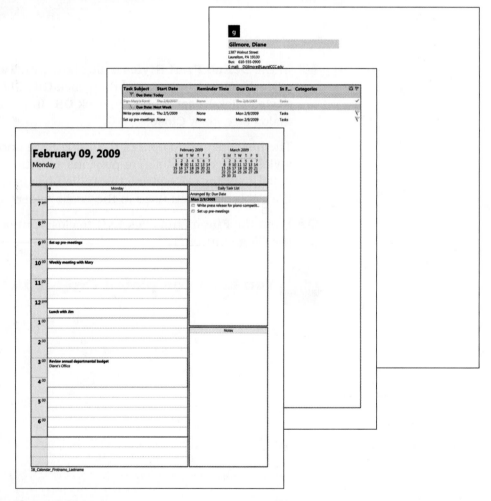

Figure 1.21
Project 1B—Personal Folders

Alert!

Complete This Project in One Working Session

Because Outlook stores information on the hard drive of the computer at which you are working, it is recommended that you schedule enough time to complete this project in one working session, unless you are working on a computer that is used only by you. Allow approximately one to two hours for Project 1B.

Objective 4
Store Contact Information

The Contacts component of Outlook is your e-mail address book for storing information about people, organizations, and businesses with which you communicate. The default location for Outlook's Contacts information is the Contacts folder.

Activity 1.10 Creating Contacts

In this activity, you will work with some existing contacts and create new contacts. A *contact* is a person or organization, inside or outside your own organization, about whom you can save information such as street and e-mail addresses, telephone and fax numbers, Web page addresses, birthdays, and even pictures. The contacts will be imported into your Contacts folder when you import Kesia Toomer's messages into your Inbox.

1 **Start** Outlook. From the **File** menu, click **Import and Export**. Under **Choose an action to perform**, make sure that **Import from another program or file** is selected, and then click **Next**.

2 Under **Select file type to import from**, click **Personal Folder File (.pst)**, and then click **Next**.

3 In the displayed **Import Personal Folders** dialog box, click **Browse**. Click the **Look in arrow** and navigate to the drive and folder to which you copied the Outlook files in Project A. Locate **01B_ Personal_Folders** and double-click it to open it. Click **Next**, and then click **Finish**. If a **Translation Warning** dialog box displays, click **OK**.

4 In the **Navigation Pane**, click **Contacts** [Contacts] to display the Contacts folder. If necessary, under Current View, click Business Cards to restore the folder to its default view.

The Contacts folder contains two existing contacts.

5 On the Standard toolbar, click the **New** button [New], click the **Maximize** button [□] if necessary, and then compare your screen with Figure 1.22.

The Untitled - Contact form displays. This form contains an area called the *Ribbon*. This toolbar contains frequently needed commands. For example, by clicking Details in the Show group, more information about a person or organization can be stored. In the General view, a blank area of the form, called the *notes area*, can be used for any information about the contact that is not otherwise specified in the form.

Figure 1.22

Untitled – Contact form   Ribbon

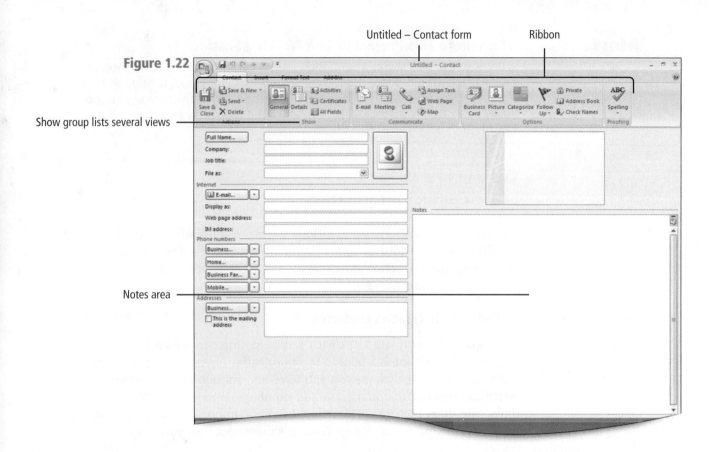

Show group lists several views

Notes area

Does your Ribbon look different?

How much information appears with each command on the Ribbon is determined by the size of the Outlook window. Users with larger screen resolutions will notice both icons and words for all commands while those with small screens may only see the icon for certain commands.

6 In the **Untitled - Contact** form, in the **Full Name** box, type **Pavel Linksz** and then press Tab.

The insertion point moves to the *Company* box, and the form title bar displays *Pavel Linksz - Contact*. Notice that the *File as* box displays the contact name as *Linksz, Pavel*. This is how it will display in the Contacts list.

7 In the **Company** box, type **Laurel County Community College** In the **Job Title** box, type **Vice President, Student Services**

8 In the **E-mail** box, type **PLinksz@LaurelCCC.edu** In the *Business Card* area, the contact data is updated as you enter information.

9 Under **Phone numbers**, in the **Business** box, click and then type **610-555-0910** Under **Addresses**, click in the **Business** box, and then type the following information on two lines: **1387 Walnut Street Laurelton, PA 19100** Click in the **Notes** area, and then compare your screen with Figure 1.23.

The Display as box shows the contact's name with the e-mail address in parentheses. When you use the contact's address in an e-mail message, this is how Outlook will display the address. Sometimes a contact's e-mail address may be completely unrelated to the person's actual name. When viewing e-mail messages, this feature helps you recall the person associated with the e-mail address.

Title bar indicates
contact name Pavel Linksz

Business Card

Figure 1.23

Contact's email
address in parentheses

Contact's name

Business Address

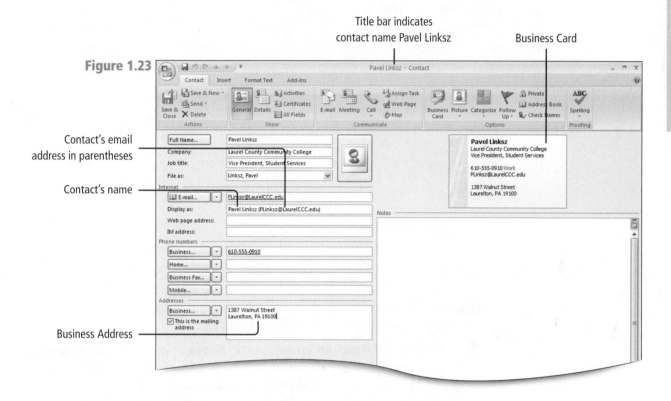

On the Ribbon in the **Actions group**, click **Save & Close** .

Outlook saves the new contact and the Contacts folder displays.

In the **Navigation Pane**, click the **Mail** button and then click **Inbox**. Click the e-mail header for the message from *Chris Horner* and hold the left mouse button down. While holding the mouse button down, drag so that the pointer is over the **Contacts** button . When the Contacts button changes color, release the left mouse button. Compare your screen with Figure 1.24.

A new Contacts form is created based on the information in the message. Notice that the name and e-mail fields are already filled out. In the Notes Pane, the original e-mail displays. This method provides a quick way to create a contact after they have sent you an e-mail.

Full name is
automatically filled in

Figure 1.24

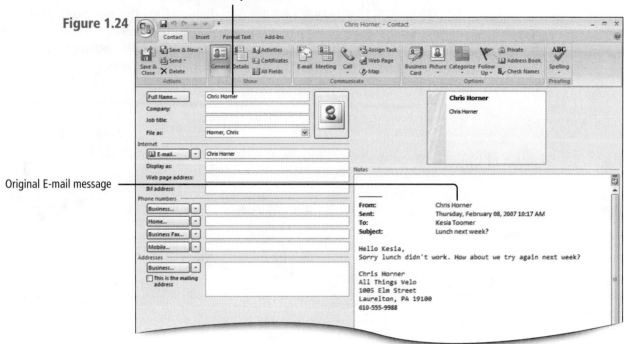

Original E-mail message

12 In the **E-mail** box, replace the existing text with
ChrisH@AllThingsVelo.com and press Tab.

13 Using the information shown in the **Notes** pane, enter the **Company**
name, **Business** phone number, and **Business** address for Chris
Horner. If necessary, minimize or maximize the Ribbon by double-
clicking the Contact tab. After entering the information, on the

Ribbon, click **Save & Close** .

14 In the **Navigation Pane**, click **Contacts** . Under
Current View, click **Address Cards**, and then compare your
Contacts list with the one displayed in Figure 1.25.

The Contacts list displays in *Address Cards* view. This view displays
certain information similar to a paper address card. Depending on
the size of your screen, the arrangement of your contacts may differ
from the figure.

Figure 1.25

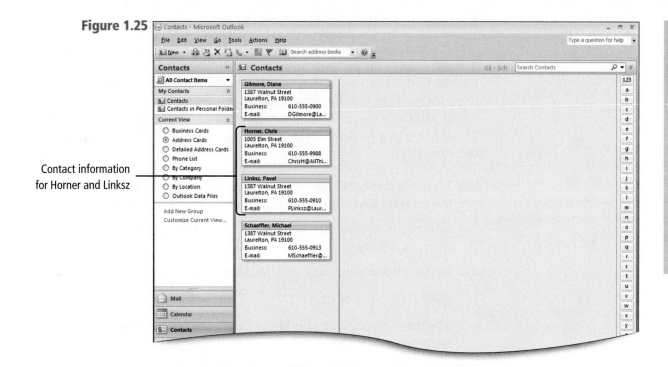

Contact information
for Horner and Linksz

More Knowledge

Verifying and Adding Information to Names, Phone Numbers, and Addresses

The Contact form contains the Full Name command button and command buttons under Phone numbers and Addresses. These command buttons display dialog boxes that enable you to add more information to a name, phone number, or address. For example, the Full Name command button displays the Check Name dialog box, in which you can add a title such as Dr. or Ms. to the contact's name. These dialog boxes also verify the accuracy of the information. Outlook displays these boxes automatically if a name, phone number, or address is incomplete or unclear.

Another Way — To Open a Blank Contact Form

You can display a blank Contact form in several ways. In addition to the toolbar button, when the Contacts folder is open you can use the keyboard shortcut Ctrl + N. Or, from the File menu, point to New, and then click Contact. Finally, you can right-click in a blank area of the Contacts folder and click New Contact on the shortcut menu.

Activity 1.11 Editing Contacts and Printing the Contacts List

When information about specific contacts changes, you can easily add details, change addresses and phone numbers, or add other information related to the contact. There may be times when you want a printed copy of your Contacts list. For example, if you are taking a business trip, you might want a printed list of the contacts you will be visiting on your trip. There are different print styles for contacts, depending on what you want to print.

1 With the **Contacts list** still displayed in *Address Cards* view, point to the contact **Chris Horner**, and then double-click to open the form.

Alternatively, point to the contact, right-click, and from the shortcut menu, click Open.

2 Under **Phone numbers**, in the **Home** box, type **610-555-0190** and then click **Save & Close** .

The new information is added to the contact, and the Contacts list redisplays.

3 With the Contacts list still in *Address Cards* view, from the **File** menu, click **Print**. Under **Print style**, click the **down scroll arrow** to view the available print styles.

Each of the different print styles arranges the contact information in a different format. You can preview how the contact information will display when you print it. Small Booklet Style and Medium Booklet Style cannot be previewed unless your selected printer supports two-sided printing.

4 Under **Print style**, click **Card Style**, and then, in the lower right corner, click **Preview**.

The preview displays the entire Contacts list in the *Card Style* print style, which displays the name and address information alphabetically by last name.

5 Point to the document, click one time to increase the magnification, use the bottom and right scroll bars to scroll as necessary, and then compare your screen with Figure 1.26.

The Card Style print style displays the information as it is currently displayed in the Contacts list, which is in the Address Cards view. Footer information may display at the bottom of the page.

Figure 1.26

Outlook | chapter 1

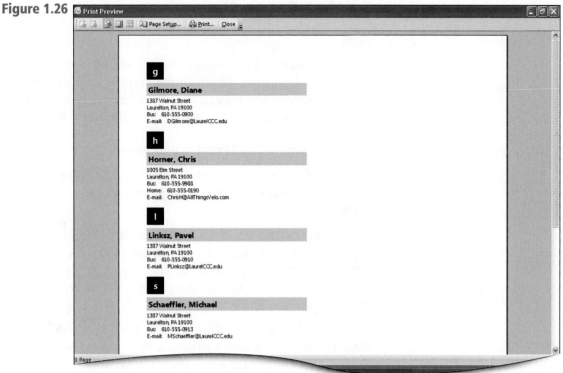

6 On the Print Preview toolbar, click the **Print** button ![Print...] to redisplay the **Print** dialog box.

7 In the **Print** dialog box, in the center of the dialog box, click **Page Setup**. In the **Options** area, locate the **Blank forms at end** box. Click the **Blank forms at end down arrow** ![down arrow], and then click **None**.

In its default setting, the Card Style print style includes a ***blank form*** page, which is a lined page added to the printout of this print style that you can use to manually list new contacts if you want to do so. You can exclude this page from the printout.

8 Click the **Header/Footer tab**, and delete any existing header or footer information, including dates and page numbers. In the left **Footer** box, using your own first and last names, type **1B_Contacts_Firstname_Lastname** Click **OK** to display the **Print** dialog box.

9 In the **Print** dialog box, click **Preview** to preview the printed document. In the **Print Preview** window, click **Print** to return to the **Print** dialog box, and then click **OK** to print the entire Contacts list.

Objective 5
Manage Tasks

In Outlook, a **_task_** is a personal or work-related activity that you want to track until it is complete. For example, writing a report, creating a memo, making a sales call, and organizing a staff meeting are all tasks. Use Outlook's Tasks component to create and manage a list of tasks.

Activity 1.12 Creating and Printing a To-Do List

You can create a new task using a Task form or enter a new task directly in the To-Do List pane. In this activity, you will edit and create tasks for Kesia Toomer.

1 In the **Navigation Pane**, click the **Tasks** button ☑ Tasks to display the **Tasks** folder. In the **To-Do List** pane, click **Sign Mary's Form**. Compare your screen with Figure 1.27. If necessary, under My Tasks, click To-Do List. If necessary, from the View menu, point to Reading Pane and click Right.

The To-Do list displays and has one task item listed. The Navigation Pane for the Tasks folder provides two views: the _To-Do List_ and _Tasks_. The **_To-Do List pane_** displays an area to type a new task and a flag for each task. A task can be flagged in several ways. Details about each task are displayed in the Reading Pane. Details include a flag for each task. To the right of the screen is the _To-Do Bar_. How your To-Do Bar displays may depend on the settings of the person who used Outlook before you.

Click to enter a new task   Task details   To-Do Bar

Figure 1.27

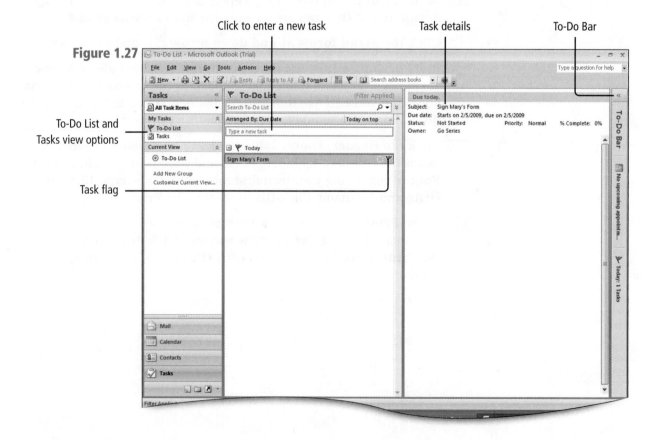

To-Do List and Tasks view options

Task flag

2 In the **To-Do List** pane, locate *Sign Mary's Form* and click its
Flag 🚩 to mark the task as completed.

The task is no longer listed in the To-Do list. Completed tasks do not
display in the To-Do list. Alternatively, select a task and on the
Standard toolbar and click the Mark Complete button or right-click
the task and select Mark Complete.

3 In the **To-Do List** pane, click in the **Type a new task** box, and then
type **Write press release for piano competition winner** Press ⏎.

The new task displays in the To-Do list. By default, the new task is
due today.

4 In the **To-Do List**, locate the header for the task just created and
double-click to open its form. Click the **Due date arrow** 🔽 and in
the calendar that displays, Click the Monday following the date you
are working on this activity. Compare your screen with Figure 1.28.
Click the **Save & Close** button 💾.

Figure 1.28

Banner indicates due
date (Yours may vary)

Your date will differ

Reminder check box cleared

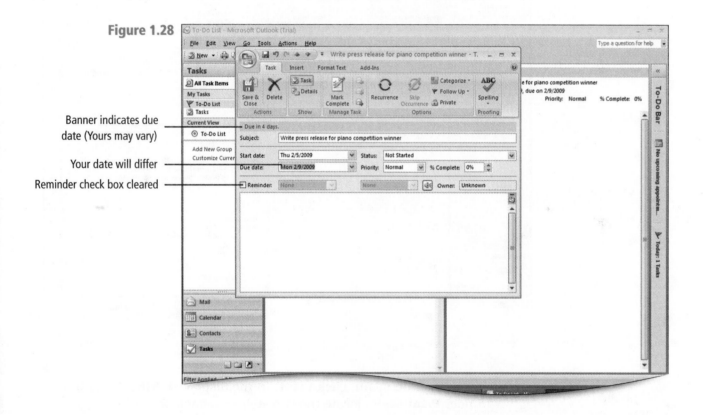

5 In the **Navigation Pane**, click the **Mail** button 📧 Mail . Locate
the message from *Diane Gilmore* with the subject, **Monthly Faculty
Meeting**. Click and drag the e-mail header on top of the **Tasks** button
📋 Tasks . When the Tasks button changes color, release the
left mouse button.

A new Task form is opened containing the information in the e-mail. This is a quick way to add a task generated from an e-mail that you have received.

6 In the **Subject** box, replace the existing text with **Set up pre-meetings**

7 Click the **Due date arrow** ⌄ and in the calendar that displays, click the Monday following the current date. Click the **Save & Close** button.

8 In the **Navigation Pane**, click **Tasks** ☑ Tasks . Click the task *Set up pre-meetings* and compare your screen with Figure 1.29.

The details for the task are displayed in the Reading Pane, including the original e-mail message.

Original e-mail message

Figure 1.29
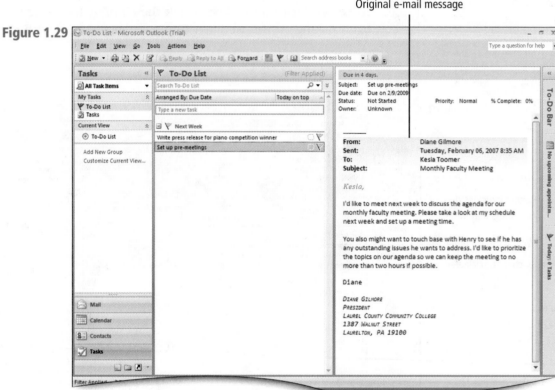

9 From the **File** menu, click **Print.** In the displayed **Print** dialog box, under **Print style**, locate the two styles available for tasks.

Memo Style is appropriate for printing individual tasks. To print the entire Tasks list, use the Table Style. Table Style is already selected as the print style.

10 In the **Print** dialog box, click **Page Setup**. In the **Page Setup: Table Style** dialog box, click the **Header/Footer tab,** and then delete any existing header or footer information, including dates and page numbers. In the left footer, using your own name, type **1B_To-Do_List_ Firstname_Lastname**

11 Click **Print Preview** to preview the printed document. In the **Print Preview** window, click **Print** [🖨 Print...] to return to the **Print** dialog box, and then click **OK** to print the To-Do list.

Objective 6
Work with the Calendar

The Calendar component of Outlook stores your schedule and calendar-related information. The default location for Outlook's calendar information is the Calendar folder. To add an item to your calendar, display this folder by clicking the Calendar button in the Navigation Pane or by clicking the Calendar folder in the Folder List.

Activity 1.13 Exploring the Calendar

In this activity, you will use the Navigation Pane and the Date Navigator to explore the calendar. These are the main tools you will use to manage Kesia Toomer's calendar activities.

1 In the **Navigation Pane**, click the **Calendar** button [▦ Calendar] and take a moment to study the main parts of the screen, as shown in Figure 1.30.

The Calendar folder displays. On the right side of the screen is the *appointment area*, which is a one-day view of the current day's calendar entries. An *appointment* is a calendar activity occurring at a specific time and day that does not require inviting other people. The *banner area* displays important calendar information including Day, Week, and Month view buttons. On each side of the appointment area are buttons that allow easy navigation to appointments that come before or after the date being viewed.

The upper pane of the Navigation Pane is the *Date Navigator*, which is a one-month view of the calendar that you can use to display specific days in a month. The highlighted date in the Date Navigator and at the top of the appointment area is the selected date that you are viewing, which is the current date by default. On each side of the appointment area are two buttons that allow quick movement to one's previous appointment or next appointment. On the Standard toolbar, the Today button changes the calendar to display the date based on your computer's system clock.

Below the appointment area is a *Task pane*, a pane that can be used to schedule tasks. Depending on your screen resolution, the Task pane may be maximized or minimized.

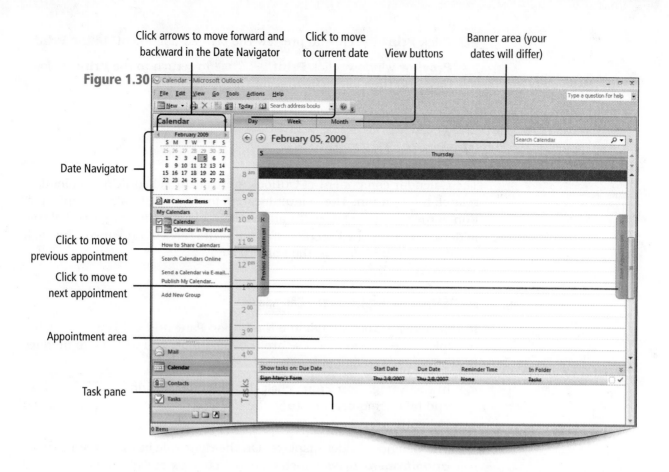

Click arrows to move forward and backward in the Date Navigator

Click to move to current date

View buttons

Banner area (your dates will differ)

Figure 1.30

Date Navigator

Click to move to previous appointment

Click to move to next appointment

Appointment area

Task pane

2 In the **Navigation Pane**, in the **Date Navigator**, click a different day of the month.

The date displayed in the appointment area changes to the day of the month you selected in the Date Navigator. In the Date Navigator, the current date remains outlined in red, and the selected date is highlighted in orange.

3 In the **Date Navigator**, click the **left arrow** ◀ next to the month name.

The Date Navigator displays the past month. The appointment area adjusts to the same day in the past month.

4 In the **Date Navigator**, click the **right arrow** ▶ several times, moving forward in the calendar two or three months.

The Date Navigator displays future months, and the appointment area adjusts to the same day in the future month.

5 On the left side of the appointment area, click the **Previous Appointment** button. An old appointment scheduled for July 7, 2006, should display in the appointment area.

6 Above the appointment area, click the **Week** button [Week]. Notice this view has two options: *Show work week* and *Show full week*.

The ***work week*** option shows only the weekdays, Monday through Friday.

7 Above the appointments area, click the **Month** button [Month]. This view provides three levels of detail: *Low*, *Medium*, and *High*.

8 Click the **Day** button [Day]. On the Standard toolbar, click the **Go to Today** button [Today] to return to the current day's calendar display.

Activity 1.14 Scheduling Appointments and Tasks

You can add a new appointment in the calendar by typing it in a blank time slot in the appointment area, by opening a blank Appointment form, or by dragging a Task into a time slot in the appointment area. In this activity, you will schedule appointments for Kesia Toomer.

1 In the **Date Navigator**, click the **Monday** following the date you are completing this activity.

2 In the appointment area, click the **10:00 am** time slot, type **Weekly meeting with Mary** and notice that as you type, the time slot is surrounded by a black border. Compare your screen with Figure 1.31.

The black border signifies that you can enter text in edit mode.

Figure 1.31

Selected Monday (your date will differ)

Appointment displays a black border as you type

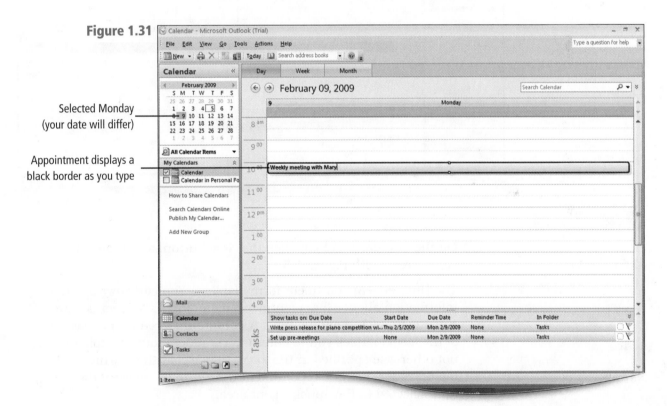

3 Click any other time slot in the appointment area.

The appointment is scheduled from 10:00 to 10:30. When you use this method to enter an appointment, Outlook automatically makes it a 30-minute appointment.

4 In the appointment area, click the **12:30 pm** time slot—that is, the lower half of the **12:00 pm** time slot—to enter an appointment on the half hour.

5 Type **Lunch with Jim** Click the **1:30 pm** time slot, and then compare your screen with Figure 1.32.

The appointment is scheduled from 12:30 to 1:00. Notice that the appointment's date in the Date Navigator changes to bold when an appointment is scheduled on that day.

Two appointments scheduled
(Your dates will differ)

Figure 1.32

Bold day number indicates an appointment is scheduled on that day

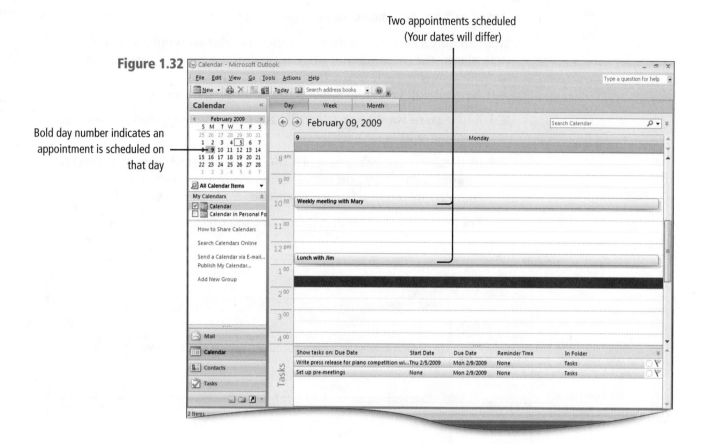

6 On the Standard toolbar, click the **New** button, and then compare your screen with Figure 1.33.

The Untitled - Appointment form displays. You can store a variety of information about an appointment, including its subject, location, starting time, and ending time. A ***comments area*** in the lower half of the form enables you to enter information about the appointment not otherwise specified in the form. Notice that the starting and ending times for the new appointment default to the current date and time selected in the appointment area.

Figure 1.33

Reminder setting

Date and time currently selected in appointment area (yours will differ)

Comments area

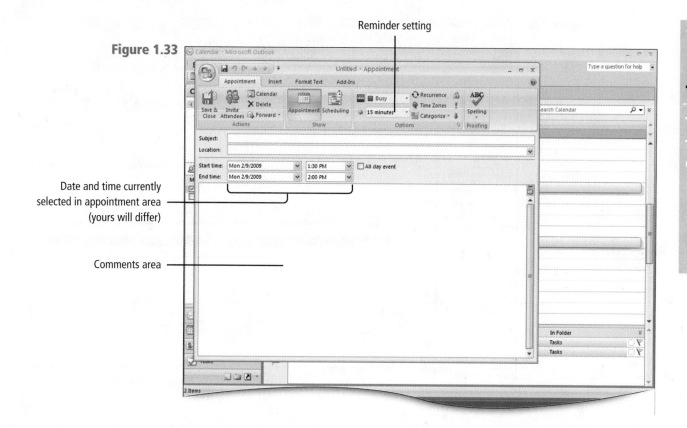

7 In the **Subject** box, type **Review annual departmental budget** In the **Location** box, type **Diane's office**

8 In the right **Start time** box, click the **arrow**, and then locate and click **3:00 PM**. In the right **End time** box, click the **arrow**, and then locate and click **4:30 PM (1.5 hours)**. On the Ribbon, click the **Reminder arrow** , and then click **None**.

A **reminder** is a small dialog box that displays in the middle of the Outlook screen to remind you of a pending appointment or task. By default, Outlook sets a reminder 15 minutes before an appointment. You can work in any Outlook folder when a reminder displays.

9 Click the **Save & Close** button , and then compare your screen with Figure 1.34. Scroll or minimize the Task pane if necessary to display the afternoon appointments.

The new appointment is added to the calendar. The appointment occupies the 3:00 to 4:30 pm time slot, and the location of the appointment displays below the item.

Figure 1.34

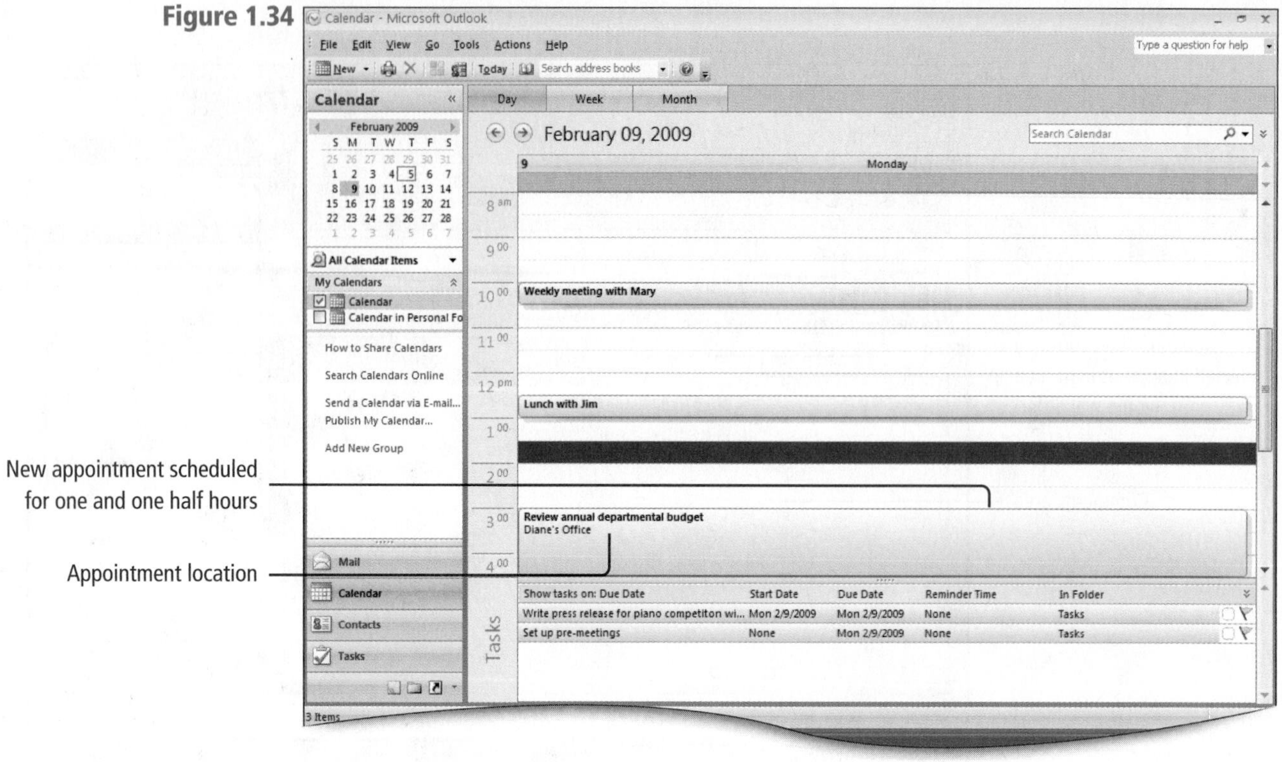

New appointment scheduled for one and one half hours

Appointment location

10 Locate the task *Set up pre-meetings*. Drag the **Set up pre-meetings** task item into the appointments area. When the pointer is in the **9:00** am time slot, release the mouse button.

A new appointment starting at 9:00 am and ending at 9:30 is created using the information in the task item.

Activity 1.15 Printing a Calendar

Depending on what you want to print in your calendar, Outlook has a variety of print styles. You can print a day, a week, or a month. You can also print an individual appointment. In this activity, you will print Kesia Toomer's daily calendar. You will then reset Outlook so that it is ready for the next user.

1 Make sure the **Monday** in the week in which you have been entering appointments is still displayed. Using the **File** menu, open the **Print** dialog box. Under **Print style**, click the **down scroll arrow** to view the available print styles.

Each print style arranges calendar information in a different format. You can preview how the information will display when you print it.

2 Under **Print style**, make sure **Daily Style** is selected, and then click **Preview**. Point to the top of the document, click one time to increase the magnification, and then compare your screen with Figure 1.35.

The *Daily Style* print style prints the appointments for the currently displayed day. It also includes the *Daily Task List*, which is an abbreviated list of current tasks stored in the Tasks folder.

Figure 1.35

Daily Style Print Style

Daily Task List

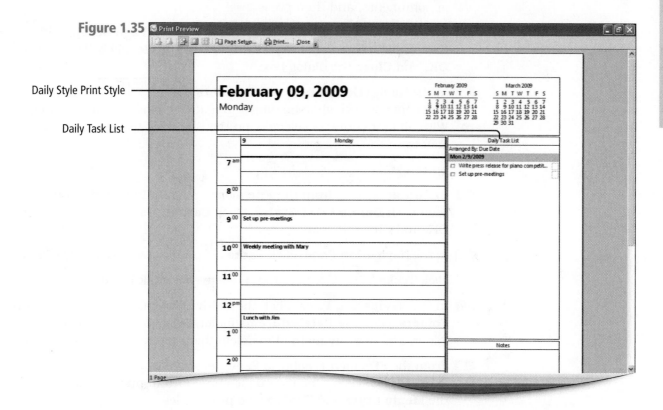

3 On the Print Preview toolbar, click the **Print** button [Print...] to redisplay the **Print** dialog box.

4 Click **Page Setup**, and then click the **Header/Footer tab.** Delete any existing header or footer information, including dates and page numbers. In the left Footer box, using your own first and last names, type **1B_Calendar_Firstname_Lastname** and then click **Print** to return to the **Print** dialog box. In the **Print** dialog box, click **OK** to print the currently displayed day.

5 In the **Navigation Pane**, click the **Mail** button [Mail] and then, under **Mail Folders**, click **Inbox**. Using the technique learned in Project 1A, delete all of the e-mail messages.

6 In the **Navigation Pane**, click **Calendar** [Calendar]. In the appointment area, click **Previous Appointment**. If necessary, click the appointment to select it and press [Delete]. Click **Next Appointment** and delete the first appointment found. Use this technique to delete all the appointments that you created in this project. Alternatively, on a day with many appointments to delete, you can select the first one, hold down [Shift], select each of the additional appointments, and then press [Delete].

7 In **Calendar** view, from the **File** menu, point to **Page Setup**, and then click **Define Print Styles**. Click **Daily Style**, click **Reset**, click **OK**, and **Close** the dialog box.

8 In the **Navigation Pane**, click **Contacts** [Contacts]. Click the first contact, and while holding [Shift] down, click the last contact. With all four contacts selected, on the Standard toolbar, click the **Delete** button [X].

9 In **Contacts** view, from the **File** menu, point to **Page Setup**, and then click **Define Print Styles**. Click **Card Style**, click **Reset**, click **OK**, and **Close** the dialog box.

10 In the **Navigation Pane**, click **Tasks** [Tasks]. Under **My Tasks**, click **Tasks** [Tasks]. Select and delete each task listed.

11 In the **Navigation Pane**, click the **Folder List** button [folder icon]. Under **All Folders**, click the **Deleted Items** folder. Select all the items in the folder, and use any method to delete them.

12 From the **File** menu, point to **Page Setup**, and then click **Define Print Styles**. Using the techniques practiced in previous steps, reset the **Memo Style** and **Table Style** print styles.

13 From the **File** menu, click **Exit** to close Outlook. Alternatively, click the **Close** button.

End **You have completed Project 1B** ————————

Content-Based Assessments

Summary

Microsoft Outlook 2007 is a personal information manager and an e-mail program. Use Outlook to manage your schedule, store information about your contacts, keep track of tasks you need to complete, and send and receive e-mail messages.

In this chapter, you practiced using Outlook's e-mail capabilities by configuring a new e-mail account, importing and reading e-mail messages, and replying to a received message. You created, edited, and printed contacts, and you created and printed a To-Do list. Finally, you scheduled some appointments in the calendar, and printed a daily schedule.

Key Terms

Content-Based Assessments

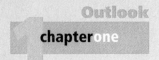
Matching

Match each term in the second column with its correct definition in the first column by writing the letter of the term on the blank line in front of the correct definition.

____ **1.** Of the two functions of Microsoft Office Outlook 2007, the function that enables you to store, electronically, information about your contact names and addresses, your calendar, and tasks you need to complete.

____ **2.** A summary view of your schedule, tasks, and e-mail for the current day—the default view when you open the Outlook program.

____ **3.** Located on the left side of the Outlook screen, a pane containing buttons and smaller panes that provides quick access to Outlook's components and folders.

____ **4.** Located on the right side of the Outlook screen when the Inbox and some other mail folders are open, a pane that allows you to read an e-mail item without actually opening it.

____ **5.** Rows of buttons from which you can perform commands with a single click of the mouse.

____ **6.** A menu of commands that displays from another menu.

____ **7.** A combination of keys on the keyboard that performs a command.

____ **8.** A tool that walks you step by step through a process.

____ **9.** Commonly used to mean in regard to or regarding.

____ **10.** The print style Outlook uses to print an individual item such as a message.

____ **11.** A person or organization, inside or outside your own organization, about whom you can save information such as street and e-mail addresses, telephone and fax numbers, Web page addresses, birthdays, and even pictures.

____ **12.** A personal or work-related activity that you want to keep track of until it is complete.

____ **13.** A calendar activity occurring at a specific time and day that does not require inviting other people.

____ **14.** A view of the calendar that you can use to display specific days in a month.

____ **15.** A print style that shows calendar appointments for the currently selected day.

A Appointment

B Contact

C Daily Style

D Date Navigator

E Keyboard shortcut

F Memo Style

G Navigation Pane

H Outlook Today

I Personal information manager

J RE

K Reading Pane

L Submenu

M Task

N Toolbars

O Wizard

Content-Based Assessments

Fill in the Blank

Write the correct answer in the space provided.

1. The _____ is the primary folder in the Mail Component.

2. Ways to look at similar Outlook information in different formats and arrangements are _____.

3. An element of information in Outlook, such as a message, a contact name, a task, or an appointment is a(n) _____.

4. The _____ _____ option in Calendar view shows five days, Monday through Friday.

5. A computer or device on a network that handles shared network resources is a(n) _____.

6. An Outlook window for displaying and collecting information is a(n) _____.

7. When your computer is connected to your organization's network or to the public Internet, it is referred to as _____.

8. A(n) _____ _____ is a combination of paper and page settings that determines the way items print.

9. You use _____ _____ to print multiple items in a folder, such as the contents of the Inbox.

10. A(n) _____ is a small dialog box that displays in the middle of the Outlook screen that tells you of a pending appointment or task.

11. A list of context-related commands that displays when you right-click a screen element is referred to as a(n) _____ _____.

12. Listed in the Inbox, a _____ _____ contains information about an e-mail message such as sender, time sent, and subject.

13. The _____ is a large toolbar that contains frequently needed commands that is available when working with forms.

14. In the Calendar folder, on the right side of the screen is the _____ _____, which is a one-day view of the current day's calendar entries.

15. In the Calendar folder, the Daily Style print style prints the appointments for the currently displayed day in addition to the _____ _____ _____, which is an abbreviated list of current tasks stored in the Tasks folder.

Content-Based Assessments

chapter one

Outlook

Skills Review

Project 1C — Career Fair

Objectives: 1. *Start and Navigate Outlook;* **2.** *Read and Respond to E-mail;* **3.** *Delete Outlook Information and Close Outlook;* **4.** *Store Contact Information;* **5.** *Manage Tasks;* **6.** *Work with the Calendar.*

In the following Skills Review, you will manage the Outlook activities for Pavel Linksz, Vice President of Student Affairs. He is setting up a career fair for students at Laurel County Community College. Your completed e-mail message, To-Do list, and schedule will look similar to the ones shown in Figure 1.36.

For Project 1C, you will need the following file:

01C_Fair

You will print
1C_Fair_Message_Firstname_Lastname
1C_Fair_Contacts_Firstname_Lastname
1C_Fair_Tasks_Firstname_Lastname
1C_Fair_Calendar_Firstname_Lastname

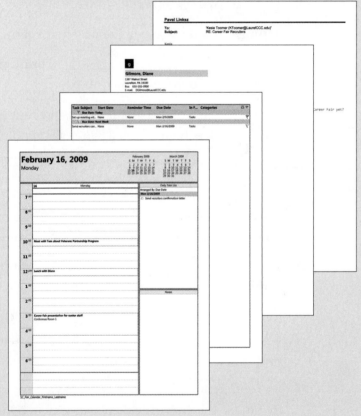

Figure 1.36
Project 1C—Career Fair

(Project 1C–Career Fair continues on the next page)

48   **Outlook** | Chapter 1: Getting Started with Outlook 2007

Content-Based Assessments

Skills Review

(Project 1C–Career Fair continued)

1. **Start** Outlook and be sure the **Navigation Pane** is displayed on the left. If necessary, to display the Navigation Pane, from the View menu, click Navigation Pane, and then click Normal.

2. You will need to have an e-mail account set up, even if you are not online. From the **Tools** menu, open the **Account Settings** dialog box. In the **Account Settings** dialog box, make sure that **E-mail** is the active tab and click **New**.

3. In the **Add New E-mail Account** dialog box, click **Next**. Click so that **Manually configure server settings** is checked, and then click **Next** two times. Enter the following:

Your Name:	Pavel Linksz
E-mail Address:	PLinksz@LaurelCCC.edu
Account Type:	POP3
Incoming mail server:	mail.LaurelCCC.edu
Outgoing mail server:	SMTP.LaurelCCC.edu
Password:	12345

   When you are done entering information, click **Next**, **Finish**, and then **Close**.

4. From the **Tools** menu, click **Options**. In the **Options** dialog box, click the **Mail Setup tab**. Under **Send/Receive**, clear the **Send immediately when connected** check box, if necessary. In the **Options** dialog box, click the **Send/Receive** button. In the **Send/Receive Groups** dialog box, under **Setting for group "All Accounts"**, clear all five check boxes, if necessary. Click **Close**, and then click **OK**.

5. From the **File** menu, display the **Import and Export Wizard** dialog box. If neces-

sary, click Import from another program or file, and then click Next. In the **Import a File** dialog box, scroll as necessary and click **Personal Folder File (.pst)**, and then click **Next**.

6. In the **Import Personal Folders** dialog box, click **Browse**. In the **Open Personal Folders** dialog box, click the **Look in arrow**.

7. In the **chapter_01_outlook** folder, click **01C_Fair** one time to select it, and then, in the lower right corner of the **Open** dialog box, click **Open**. Click **Next**. Click **Finish**. If a **Translation Warning** dialog box displays, click **OK**. Mail items are placed in your Inbox.

8. In the lower portion of the **Navigation Pane**, click the **Mail** button to display the Mail folders, and then, at the top of the pane, click **Inbox** to display the Inbox folder.

9. In the **Inbox**, select the message header with the subject **Career Fair Recruiters**. Then, on the Standard toolbar, click the **Reply** button.

10. With the insertion point at the top of the message area, type **Kesia,** and press Enter two times. Type **I am working on it now. I will send it to you by the end of the day.** Press Enter two times, and type **Pavel** On the Ribbon, click the **Send** button.

11. In the **Navigation Pane**, under **Mail Folders**, click **Outbox** to display the Outbox folder. Click the **RE: Career Fair Recruiters** message in the Outbox one time to select it. From the **File** menu, click **Print**, and then click **Page Setup**. In the **Page Setup: Memo Style** dialog box, click the **Header/Footer tab**. Under **Footer**,

(Project 1C–Career Fair continues on the next page)

Content-Based Assessments

Skills Review

(Project 1C–Career Fair continued)

delete any existing header or footer information. In the left **Footer** box, using your own name, type **1C_Fair_Message_Firstname_Lastname** and click **Print Preview**.

12. In the **Print Preview** window, click **Print** to return to the **Print** dialog box, and then click **OK** to print the message. In the **Outbox**, with the **RE: Career Fair Recruiters** message still selected, on the Standard toolbar, click the **Delete** button to delete the message.

13. In the **Navigation Pane**, click **Contacts**. On the Standard toolbar, click the **New** button. In the **Untitled – Contact** form, enter the following information using your own name and school name. Click **Save & Close** when you are done.

Full Name **Firstname Lastname**
Company **Your school's name**
E-mail **Firstname_Lastname@college.edu**

14. In the **Navigation Pane**, under **Current View**, click **Business Cards** if necessary. From the **File** menu, open the **Print** dialog box. With the **Card Style** print style selected, click **Page Setup**. On the **Format** tab, under **Options**, change **Blank forms at end** to **None**. Click the **Header/Footer tab**. Remove all header and footer text. In the left **Footer** box, type **1C_Fair_Contacts_Firstname_Lastname** Click **OK** two times to print the contacts.

15. In the **Navigation Pane**, click the **Tasks** button to display the Tasks folder. On the Standard toolbar, click the **New** button. In the **Untitled - Task** form, in the **Subject** box, type **Send recruiters confirmation letters** Click the **Due date arrow**. On the displayed calendar, click a date one week from the current date. Clear the **Reminder**

check box if necessary, and then click **Save & Close**.

16. Click the **Mail** button, and then click **Inbox**. Locate the e-mail header with the subject **Student Veterans and the Career Fair**. Drag the message header until the pointer is over the **Tasks** button. When the **Tasks** button changes color, release the mouse. In the **Subject**, replace the existing text with **Set up meeting with Tom** Set the **Due date** to the current date, and then click **Save & Close**.

17. In the **Navigation Pane**, click **Tasks**. From the **File** menu, click **Print**. In the **Print** dialog box, click **Page Setup**. Click the **Header/Footer tab**, and then delete any existing header or footer information. In the left **Footer** box, using your own name, type **1C_Fair_Tasks_Firstname_Lastname** Click the **Print Preview** button to preview the printed document. In the **Print Preview** window, click **Print**, and then click **OK** to print the To-Do list.

18. In the **Navigation Pane**, click the **Calendar** button. In the **Date Navigator**, click the **Monday** of the next week.

19. In the appointment area, click the **10:00 am** time slot, type **Meet with Tom about Veterans Partnership Program** Click the **12:00 pm** time slot and type **Lunch with Diane** Click any blank time slot in the appointment area.

20. On the Standard toolbar, click the **New** button. As the **Subject** of the appointment, type **Career Fair presentation for senior staff** In the **Location** box, type **Conference Room 1** To the right of the **Start time** box, click the **down arrow**, and then locate and click **3:00 PM**. To the right of the **End time** box, click the **down arrow**, and then locate and click **4:30 PM**

(Project 1C–Career Fair continues on the next page)

Content-Based Assessments

(Project 1C–Career Fair continued)

(1.5 hours). On the Ribbon, in the **Options** area, use the **Reminder** spin box to set the reminder to **None**. Click **Save & Close**.

21. From the **File** menu, click **Print**. Make sure **Daily Style** is the selected **Print style**, and then click **Page Setup**. Click the **Header/Footer tab**. Delete any existing header or footer information, including dates and page numbers. In the left **Footer** box, using your own first and last names, type 1C_Fair_Calendar_ Firstname_Lastname and then click **Print** to return to the **Print** dialog box. In the **Print** dialog box, click **OK** to print the calendar's currently displayed day.

22. Click the **Meet with Tom about Veterans Partnership Program** appointment, press ⇧ Shift, and then click the two remaining appointments. Click **Delete** to delete all the appointments for that day. In the **Navigation Pane**, click **Tasks**, and then delete both tasks. Click **Mail**, display the **Inbox**, and delete the two messages. Click **Contacts** and delete all of the contacts.

23. Click the **Deleted Items** folder. Select the first item in the folder, press ⇧ Shift, select the last item in the folder, and then click **Delete**. In the **Microsoft Office Outlook** dialog box, click **Yes** to permanently delete the items and empty the folder.

24. In the **Navigation Pane**, click the **Mail** button. From the **Tools** menu, display the **Options** dialog box, and then click the **Mail Setup tab**. Under **Send/Receive**, select the **Send immediately when connected** check box. Then, to the right of the check box, click the **Send/Receive** button. In the **Send/Receive Groups** dialog box, click to select both **Include this group in send/receive (F9)** check boxes. Under **Setting for group "All Accounts"**, click to select **Schedule an automatic send/receive**. Click **Close**, and then click **OK**.

25. From the **Tools** menu, open the **Account Settings** dialog box. Select the account you created for *PLinksz* and click **Remove**. Outlook asks if you want to delete the account. Click **Yes**, and then **Close** the dialog box.

26. From the **Mail** view, click the **File** menu, point to **Page Setup**, and then click **Define Print Styles**. Click **Memo Style**, click **Reset**, and then click **OK**. Repeat this technique to **Reset** the **Table Style** print style and **Close** the Page Setup dialog box. Using the previous techniques, change to **Contacts** view and **Reset** the **Card Style** print style. Change to **Calendar** view and **Reset** the **Daily Style** print style.

27. On the Outlook title bar, click the **Close** button.

End You have completed Project 1C

Content-Based Assessments

Mastering Outlook

Project 1D — Network Consultant

Objectives: 1. *Start and Navigate Outlook;* **2.** *Read and Respond to E-mail;* **3.** *Delete Outlook Information and Close Outlook;* **4.** *Store Contact Information;* **5.** *Manage Tasks;* **6.** *Work with the Calendar.*

In the following Mastering Outlook project, you will create contacts and a schedule, and reply to an e-mail message for Kesia Toomer, the Vice President of Administration and Development at Laurel County Community College. Kesia is directing the consultants through an upgrade of the computer network in the Administration building. Your completed Contacts list, message, and schedule will look similar to the ones shown in Figure 1.37.

For Project 1D, you will need the following file:

01D_Network

You will print
1D_Network_Contacts_Firstname_Lastname
1D_Network_Message_Firstname_Lastname
1D_Network_Calendar_Firstname_Lastname

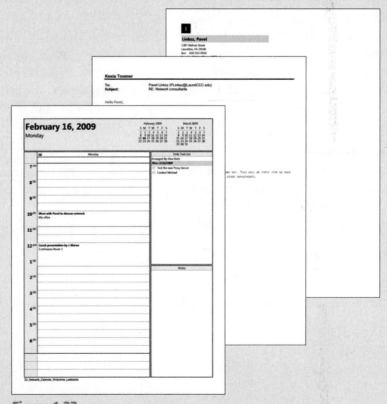

Figure 1.37
Project 1D—Network Consultant

(Project 1D–Network Consultant continues on the next page)

Content-Based Assessments

(Project 1D—Network Consultant continued)

1. **Start** Outlook. Use the **Account Settings** dialog box to create a new e-mail account. In the **Add New E-mail Account** dialog box, for **Choose E-mail Service**, click **Next**. For **Account Basics**, select **Manually configure server settings**, and then click **Next**. For **Choose E-mail Service**, select **Internet E-mail**, and then click **Next**. For **Internet E-mail Settings**, enter the following:

Your Name:	Kesia Toomer
E-mail Address:	KToomer@LaurelCCC.edu
Incoming mail server:	mail.LaurelCCC.edu
Outgoing mail server:	SMTP.LaurelCCC.edu
User Name:	KToomer
Password:	12345

When you are done entering information, complete the Add New E-mail Account process, and then **Close** the Account Settings dialog box.

2. Open the **Options** dialog box. On the **Mail Setup** tab, clear the **Send immediately when connected** check box, if necessary. Open the **Send/Receive Groups** dialog box and under **Setting for group "All Accounts"**, clear all five check boxes if necessary. Close all dialog boxes.

3. Using the technique learned in previous projects, import the Personal Folder File (.*pst*) **01D_Network**, located with the files that you copied from the **chapter_01_outlook** folder.

4. Add the following items to the **Contacts** folder with the following information:

   Pavel Linksz
   Laurel County Community College
   Vice President, Student Services
   610-555-0910
   1387 Walnut Street
   Laurelton, PA 19100
   PLinksz@LaurelCCC.edu

   Jason Moran
   Park Associates Network Solutions, Inc.
   610-555-0189
   333 Grand Avenue
   Laurelton, PA 19109
   JMoran@parkassociates.com

5. Set the **Contacts** list to print with the following settings:
   Current View: Business Cards
   Print style: Card Style
   Blank forms at end: None

   In the left **Footer** box, using your own name, type **1D_Network_Contacts_Firstname_Lastname** Delete all other header and footer information. When you are done, preview and print the Contacts list.

6. Reply to the **Network consultants** e-mail message from *Pavel Linksz*. In the message area, type **Hello Pavel,** Press [Enter] two times, and then type **I will let you know how Park Associates works out as we get into the project.** Press [Enter] two times, and then type **Kesia**

(Project 1D—Network Consultant continues on the next page)

(Project 1D–Network Consultant continued)

7. Send the message. In the **Outbox**, set the message you just created to print in **Memo Style** with the following left footer: **1D_Network_Message_Firstname_Lastname** Delete all other header and footer information. Preview and print the message and then delete the contents of the **Outbox**.

8. Create a new task with the following information:

Subject: **Test the new Proxy Server**
Due date: **The Monday following today's date**
Reminder: **None**

When you are done, **Save** and **Close** the task.

9. Locate the message with the subject *Please contact Michael*. Create a new task by dragging the e-mail into the **Tasks** folder. Change the Subject to **Contact Michael** set the Due date to the Monday following today's date, and save and close the task.

10. For the Monday following today's date, create two appointments with the following information:

Subject: **Meet with Pavel to discuss network**
Location: **My office**
Start time: 10:00 am
End time: 11:00 am
Reminder: None
Subject: **Lunch presentation by J Moran**
Location: **Conference Room 1**
Start time: 12:00 pm
End time: 1:30 pm
Reminder: None

11. For the Monday following today's date, print the daily schedule with the following settings:

Print Style: Daily Style

Left Footer: **1D_Network_Calendar_Firstname_Lastname**

Delete all other header and footer information, and then preview and print the calendar.

12. Delete the calendar entries and tasks for the day in which you have been working. Delete all the contacts that you created. Delete all the items in the **Inbox**. Finally, delete all items in the **Deleted Items** folder.

13. Open the **Options** dialog box. Click the **Mail Setup tab**, and under **Send/Receive**, select the **Send immediately when connected** check box. Click **Send/Receive**. In the **Send/Receive Groups** dialog box, under **Setting for group "All Accounts"**, select both **Include this group in send/receive (F9)** check boxes. Under **Setting for group "All Accounts"**, select **Schedule an automatic send/receive**. Click **Close**, and then click **OK**.

14. Use the **Account Settings** dialog box to delete the account for *Kesia Toomer*.

15. Reset the following Print Styles: Memo Style, Card Style, and Daily Style. (Hint: Card Style appears when in Contacts view and Daily Style appears when in Calendar view.)

16. Close Outlook.

 End **You have completed Project 1D**

Mastering Outlook

Project 1E—Staff Party

Objectives: 1. *Start and Navigate Outlook;* **2.** *Read and Respond to E-mail;* **3.** *Delete Outlook Information and Close Outlook;* **4.** *Store Contact Information;* **5.** *Manage Tasks;* **6.** *Work with the Calendar.*

In the following Mastering Outlook project, you will manage the Outlook activities for Mary Adair, who works for Kesia Toomer, Vice President of Administration and Development at Laurel County Community College. Kesia has asked Mary to organize a staff party for the administrative staff. You will reply to e-mail, create contacts and a To-Do list, and schedule appointments in Mary's calendar. Your completed Contacts list, Tasks list, and calendar will look similar to the one shown in Figure 1.38.

For Project 1E, you will need the following file:

01E_Party

You will print
1E_Party_E-mail_Firstname_Lastname
1E_Party_Contacts_Firstname_Lastname
1E_Party_Tasks_Firstname_Lastname
1E_Party_Calendar_Firstname_Lastname

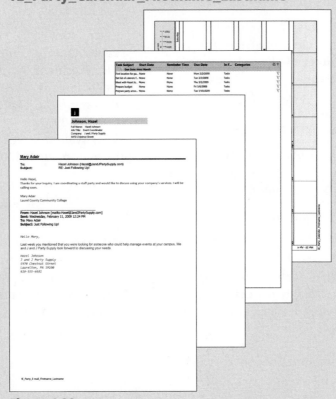

Figure 1.38
Project 1E—Staff Party
(Project 1E–Staff Party continues on the next page)

Mastering Outlook

(Project 1E–Staff Party continued)

1. **Start** Outlook. Use the **Account Settings** dialog box to create a new e-mail account. In the **Add New E-mail Account** dialog box, for **Choose E-mail Service**, and then click **Next**. For **Account Basics**, select **Manually configure server settings**, and then click **Next**. For **Choose E-mail Service**, select **Internet E-mail**, and then click **Next**. For **Internet E-mail Settings**, enter the following:

   Your Name: **Mary Adair**
   E-mail Address: **MAdair@LaurelCCC.edu**
   Incoming mail server: **mail.LaurelCCC.edu**
   Outgoing mail server: **SMTP.LaurelCCC.edu**
   User Name: **MAdair**
   Password: **12345**

   When you are done entering information, complete the Add New E-mail Account process, and then **Close** the Account Settings dialog box.

2. Open the **Options** dialog box, click the **Mail Setup tab**, and clear the **Send immediately when connected** check box if necessary. Open the **Send/Receive Groups** dialog box and under **Setting for group "All Accounts"**, clear all five check boxes, if necessary. **Close** all dialog boxes.

3. Import the Personal Folder File (.pst) **01E_Party** located with the files you copied from the **chapter_01_outlook** folder.

4. Reply to the e-mail from *Hazel Johnson* using the following message:

   Hello Hazel,
   Thanks for your inquiry. I am coordinating a staff party and would like to discuss using your company's services. I will be calling soon.

   Mary Adair
   Laurel County Community College

   Send the message.

5. Prepare to print the e-mail message that you just sent to *Hazel Johnson*. Apply the **Memo Style** with a left footer **1E_Party_E-mail_Firstname_Lastname** Delete all other header and footer information. Preview and print the message and then delete the message from the **Outbox**.

6. Using the e-mail from *Hazel Johnson*, create a new contact by dragging it into the **Contacts** folder. In the **Contact** form, use the information found in the **Notes** area to enter the Company name, Business Phone number, and Business Address. Leave the e-mail message in the Notes area. When you are done entering information, Save and Close the contact item.

7. Create a new Contact item with the following information:

   Kesia Toomer
   Laurel County Community College
   Vice President, Administration and Development
   KToomer@LaurelCCC.edu
   610-555-0911
   1387 Walnut Street
   Laurelton, PA 19100

   When you are done entering information, Save and Close the contact item.

8. Display the Contacts list in **Detailed Address Card** view. Prepare to print the Contacts list in **Card Style** with the left footer **1E_Party_Contacts_Firstname_Lastname** Set the **Blank forms at end** to **None**. Preview and print the Contacts list.

(Project 1E–Staff Party continues on the next page)

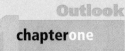

(Project 1E–Staff Party continued)

9. Create five new task items, using the following information:

Subject	Due Date
Find location for party	The first Monday of next month
Get list of caterers from Don	The first Tuesday of next month
Meet with Hazel Johnson about decorations	The first Thursday of next month
Prepare budget	The first Friday of next month
Prepare party announcement	The second Tuesday of next month

10. Prepare to print the **To-Do list** in **Table Style** with the footer 1E_Party_Tasks_ Firstname_Lastname Preview and print the To-Do list.

11. Display the appointments for the *first* Friday of next month. In the **Tasks** pane located below the appointments area, locate the task *Prepare budget*. Use the drag-and-drop method to schedule time for this task on that Friday. Set the starting time at 11:30 am and ending time at 12:30 pm.

12. For the *third* Friday of next month, create three new appointments, clearing the reminders for each: **Meet with caterers** in **My office** starting at 10:00 am and ending at 11:00 am; **Party setup** in **Restaurant banquet room** starting at 2:00 pm and ending at 3:00 pm; and **Staff Party** starting at 4:00 pm and ending at 6:00 pm.

13. With the third Friday of next month still displayed, prepare to print the calendar for next month in **Monthly Style** with the footer 1E_Party_Calendar_Firstname_Lastname Clear all other footer information. Preview and print the calendar.

14. Delete all of the appointments that you created. Delete the contents of the **Contacts** folder, and then restore the **Current View** to **Business Cards**. Delete the contents of the **Tasks** folder. Delete the contents of the **Inbox**, and then empty the **Deleted Items** folder.

15. Reset the following **Print Styles** to their defaults: **Memo Style**, **Table Style**, **Monthly Style**, and **Card Style**.

16. Open the **Options** dialog box. Click the **Mail Setup tab**, and under **Send/Receive**, select the **Send immediately when connected** check box. Click **Send/Receive**. In the **Send/Receive Groups** dialog box, under **Setting for group "All Accounts"**, select both **Include this group in send/receive (F9)** check boxes. Under **Setting for group "All Accounts"**, click to check **Schedule an automatic send/receive**. Click **Close**, and then click **OK**.

17. Use the **Account Settings** dialog box to delete the account for *Mary Adair*. **Close** Outlook.

End You have completed Project 1E

Mastering Outlook

Project 1F—Administration

Objectives: 1. *Start and Navigate Outlook;* **2.** *Read and Respond to E-mail;* **3.** *Delete Outlook Information and Close Outlook;* **5.** *Manage Tasks;* **6.** *Work with the Calendar.*

In the following Mastering Outlook project, you will manage administrative activities for Kesia Toomer, Vice President of Administration and Development at Laurel County Community College. You will import her messages into the Inbox, reply to several messages, and create a To-Do list. Your completed messages and To-Do list will look similar to the ones shown in Figure 1.39.

For Project 1F, you will need the following file:

01F_Admin

You will print
1F_PR_Message_Firstname_Lastname
1F_Presentation_Message_Firstname_Lastname
1F_Admin_Tasks_Firstname_Lastname
1F_Admin_Calendar_Firstname_Lastname

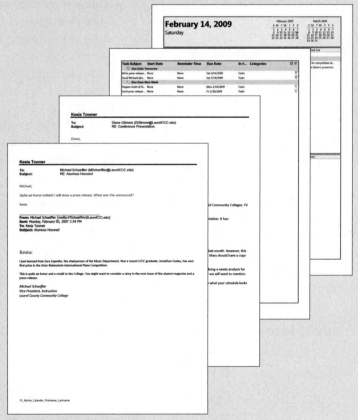

Figure 1.39
Project 1F—Administration

(Project 1F–Administration continues on the next page)

Content-Based Assessments

Mastering Outlook

(Project 1F–Administration continued)

1. **Start** Outlook. Use the **Account Settings** dialog box to create a new e-mail account. In the **Add New E-mail Account** dialog box, for **Choose E-mail Service**, and then click **Next**. For **Account Basics**, select **Manually configure server settings**, and then click **Next**. For **Choose E-mail Service**, select **Internet E-mail**, and then click **Next**. For **Internet E-mail Settings**, enter the following:

   Your Name: **Kesia Toomer**
   E-mail Address: **KToomer@LaurelCCC.edu**
   Incoming mail server: **mail.LaurelCCC.edu**
   Outgoing mail server: **SMTP.LaurelCCC.edu**
   User Name: **KToomer**
   Password: **12345**

   When you are done entering information, complete the Add New E-mail Account process and **Close** the Account Settings dialog box.

2. Open the **Options** dialog box, click the **Mail Setup tab** and clear the **Send immediately when connected** check box, if necessary. Open the **Send/Receive Groups** dialog box and under **Setting for group "All Accounts"**, clear all five check boxes if necessary. **Close** all dialog boxes.

3. Import the Personal Folder File (.pst) **01F_Admin** located with the files you copied from the **chapter_01_outlook** folder.

4. Locate the e-mail with the subject *Alumnus honored*. Reply to the e-mail using the following information. Use appropriate spacing as shown in Figure 1.39:

   Michael, Quite an honor indeed! I will issue a press release. When was this announced? Kesia

5. Send the message. Reply to the e-mail with the subject *Conference Presentation* using the following information.

Use appropriate spacing as shown in Figure 1.39:

Diane, I can start working on this right away. Let's plan on meeting next Monday. Kesia

6. Send the message. In the **Outbox**, for the message with the subject *RE: Alumnus honored*, set the message to print in **Memo Style** with the footer **1F_PR_Message_Firstname_Lastname** Preview and print the message.

7. In the **Outbox**, for the message with the subject *RE: Conference Presentation*, set the message to print in **Memo Style** with the footer **1F_Presentation_Message_Firstname_Lastname** Preview and print the message.

8. Create four new tasks, using the following information:

Subject	Due Date
Write press release for competition winner	Tomorrow
Send press release to alumni magazine editor	Next Friday
Prepare draft of Diane's presentation	Next Monday
E-mail Michael about Diane's presentation	Tomorrow

9. Set the **To-Do list** to print in **Table Style** with the footer **1F_Admin_Tasks_Firstname_Lastname** Preview and print the To-Do list.

10. In the **Calendar** view, display tomorrow in the appointment area. Using drag and drop, schedule the following times for the two items in the Task pane:

Write press release for competition winner	9:00 am to 10:00 am
E-mail Michael about Diane's presentation	10:00 am to 10:30 am

(Project 1F–Administration continues on the next page)

Content-Based Assessments

Mastering Outlook

(Project 1F–Administration continued)

11. Prepare to print the calendar for tomorrow in **Daily Style** with the footer 1F_Admin_Calendar_Firstname_Lastname Clear all other footer information. Preview and print the calendar.

12. Delete the contents of the **Outbox**, **Inbox**, **Calendar**, and **Tasks** folders and then empty the **Deleted Items** folder.

13. Reset the **Memo Style**, **Table Style**, and **Daily Style** print styles to their defaults.

14. Open the **Options** dialog box. Click the **Mail Setup tab**, and under **Send/Receive**, select the **Send immediately**

when connected check box. Click **Send/Receive**. In the **Send/Receive Groups** dialog box, under **Setting for group "All Accounts"**, select both **Include this group in send/receive (F9)** check boxes. Under **Setting for group "All Accounts"**, click to check **Schedule an automatic send/receive.** Click **Close**, and then click **OK**.

15. Use the **Account Settings** dialog box to delete the account for *Kesia Toomer*. **Close** Outlook.

End **You have completed Project 1F** ──────────────

Rubric

The following outcomes-based assessments are *open-ended assessments*. That is, there is no specific correct result; your result will depend on your approach to the information provided. Make *Professional Quality* your goal. Use the following scoring rubric to guide you in *how* to approach the problem and then to evaluate *how well* your approach solves the problem.

The *criteria*—Software Mastery, Content, Format and Layout, and Process—represent the knowledge and skills you have gained that you can apply to solving the problem. The *levels of performance*—Professional Quality, Approaching Professional Quality, or Needs Quality Improvements—help you and your instructor evaluate your result.

	Your completed project is of Professional Quality if you:	Your completed project is Approaching Professional Quality if you:	Your completed project Needs Quality Improvements if you:
1-Software Mastery	Choose and apply the most appropriate skills, tools, and features and identify efficient methods to solve the problem.	Choose and apply some appropriate skills, tools, and features, but not in the most efficient manner.	Choose inappropriate skills, tools, or features, or are inefficient in solving the problem.
2-Content	Construct a solution that is clear and well organized, contains content that is accurate, appropriate to the audience and purpose, and is complete. Provide a solution that contains no errors of spelling, grammar, or style.	Construct a solution in which some components are unclear, poorly organized, inconsistent, or incomplete. Misjudge the needs of the audience. Have some errors in spelling, grammar, or style, but the errors do not detract from comprehension.	Construct a solution that is unclear, incomplete, or poorly organized, containing some inaccurate or inappropriate content; and contains many errors of spelling, grammar, or style. Do not solve the problem.
3-Format and Layout	Format and arrange all elements to communicate information and ideas, clarify function, illustrate relationships, and indicate relative importance.	Apply appropriate format and layout features to some elements, but not others. Overuse features, causing minor distraction.	Apply format and layout that does not communicate information or ideas clearly. Do not use format and layout features to clarify function, illustrate relationships, or indicate relative importance. Use available features excessively, causing distraction.
4-Process	Use an organized approach that integrates planning, development, self-assessment, revision, and reflection.	Demonstrate an organized approach in some areas, but not others; or, use an insufficient process of organization throughout.	Do not use an organized approach to solve the problem.

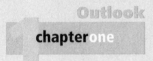

Problem Solving

Project 1G — Child Center

In this project, you will construct a solution by applying any combination of the Objectives found in Projects 1A and 1B.

For Project 1G, you will need the following file:

01G_Center

**You will print
1G_Reply_Firstname_Lastname**

Laurel County Community College operates a fully staffed child development center for use by its students, faculty, and staff. Because of the college's large adult education program, the center is an important resource for students. The director of the child development center reports to Kesia Toomer, Vice President of Administration and Development. Compose an e-mail message from her to Pavel Linksz, Vice President of Student Services. Dr. Linksz is requesting information about the child development center that will be included in the student packet for incoming adult students. Ms. Toomer's reply needs to describe the facility, staff, and hours of operation of the center.

Create a new e-mail account with the following settings:

Your Name: **Kesia Toomer**
E-mail Address: **KToomer@LaurelCCC.edu**
Incoming mail server: **mail.LaurelCCC.edu**
Outgoing mail server: **SMTP.LaurelCCC.edu**
User Name: **KToomer**
Password: **12345**

Configure the Send/Receive settings so that the sent messages will be placed in the Outbox instead of the Sent Items folder. Import the file 01G_Center.

Locate the message from Pavel Linksz about the Child Development Center. Compose a reply to the message. For the text of the message, write three paragraphs of general information—an introductory paragraph describing the facility, a second paragraph describing the staff, and a third paragraph that covers the hours of operation. Close the message using the name Kesia. Suggestion: To help you compose your paragraphs, visit the Web site of your college to see whether it has a child development center. Or go to *www.pasadena.edu* and follow the links to Student Services, and then to their Child Development Center.

(Project 1G–Child Center continues on the next page)

Outcomes-Based Assessments

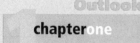
Problem Solving

(Project 1G–Child Center continued)

From the Outbox, print the message, using the Memo Style print style with **1G_Reply_Firstname_Lastname** in the left footer.

Delete the contents of the Inbox and Outbox, and then empty the Deleted Items folder. Reset the Memo Style to its default settings. Delete the account that you created for Kesia Toomer. Restore the Send/Receive options to their default settings.

End **You have completed Project 1G** ⸺⸺⸺⸺⸺⸺⸺⸺⸺⸺⸺

Project 1H—Athletic Center Dedication

In this project, you will construct a solution by applying any combination of the Objectives found in Projects 1A and 1B.

For Project 1H, you will need the following file:

None

You will print
1H_Tasks_Firstname_Lastname
1H_Contacts_Firstname_Lastname
1H_Calendar_Firstname_Lastname

Pavel Linksz, Vice President of Student Services at Laurel County Community College, is preparing the dedication ceremony for a new student athletic center. On the calendar, display the next Saturday, which will be the day of the dedication. Removing all reminders, schedule an appointment for the setup for the ceremony, and then schedule the ceremony itself. Schedule a reception following the dedication. Print that day's schedule with the left footer as **1H_Calendar_Firstname_Lastname** Delete the calendar entries.

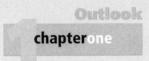

Outlook
chapterone

Problem Solving

(Project 1H–Athletic Center Dedication continued)

Create a To-Do list for at least seven new tasks related to the dedication ceremony of the athletic center. Possible tasks might include arranging for speakers, reserving audio equipment, ordering refreshments, notifying the local press, and inviting important guests. Print the To-Do list in Table Style with the left footer as
1H_Tasks_Firstname_Lastname

Create at least four new contacts related to the dedication. Create fictitious contacts for a reporter at a local newspaper, a photographer, a caterer, and a printing company. Display the Contacts list in Detailed Address Cards view and then print the Contacts list in Card Style with the left footer as **1H_Contacts_Firstname_Lastname**

Restore the Contacts folder to its default view and delete the contents of the folder. Delete the contents of the Tasks folder, and empty the Deleted Items folder. Reset the print styles you used when you printed the calendar, To-Do list, and Contacts list.

End **You have completed Project 1H** —————————————————————

GO! with Help

Project 1I—*GO!* with Help

The Outlook Help system can help you as you work. In the following steps, you will view information about getting help as you work in Outlook.

1 Start **Outlook**. In the **Type a question for help** box, type **How can I print a Help topic?** and press Enter.

2 In the **Outlook Help** window, click **Print a Help topic**. A Microsoft Office Outlook Help window explains how to print the information found in a Help window.

3 Follow the directions in the Help window to print its contents. Your name will not display on this printout.

4 **Close** the Help window and then **Close** Outlook.

End **You have completed Project 1I** —————————————————————

Glossary

Adaptive A feature where menus adapt to the way you work by displaying the commands you most frequently use.

Appointment A calendar activity occurring at a specific time and day that does not require inviting other people.

Appointment area A one-day view of the current day's calendar entries.

Banner area The screen area that displays important calendar information including *Day*, *Week*, and *Month* view buttons.

Blank form A lined page added to the printout of the Card print style that you can use to manually list new contacts.

Card Style A print style which displays the name and address information alphabetically by last name.

Comments area The area in the lower half of the Appointments form and Task form where you can enter information not otherwise specified in the form.

Contact A person or organization about whom you can save information such as street and e-mail addresses, telephone and fax numbers, Web page addresses, birthdays, and even pictures.

Daily Style A print style that prints the appointments for the currently displayed day.

Daily Task List An abbreviated list of current tasks stored in the Tasks folder.

Date Navigator A one-month view of the calendar that you can use to display specific days in a month.

E-Mail Account A unique address that you can use to receive and send e-mail.

Form A window for displaying and collecting information.

Icon A graphic representation of an object that you can click to open that object.

Inbox The folder that stores e-mail.

Items An element of information in Outlook, such as a message, a contact name, a task, or an appointment.

Keyboard shortcut A combination of keys on the keyboard that perform a command.

Memo Style A print style that prints a single item on a single page and provides detailed information about that item.

Menu A list of commands within a category.

Message header The basic information about an e-mail message such as the sender's name, the date sent, and the subject.

Microsoft Exchange Server An e-mail based communications server for businesses and organizations.

Navigation Pane The area on the left side of the Outlook window that provides quick access to Outlook's components.

Notes area A blank area of the Contact form that can be used for any information about the contact that is not otherwise specified in the form.

Offline Your status when you are not connected to a network or to the public Internet.

Online Your status when you are connected to your organization's network or to the public Internet.

Outlook Today A summary view of your schedule, tasks, and e-mail for the current day.

Personal information manager A feature that enables you to electronically store and manage information about contacts, appointments, and tasks.

Print styles A combination of paper and page settings that determines the way items print.

RE Commonly used to mean *in regard to* or *regarding*.

Reading Pane A window in which you can preview an e-mail message without actually opening it.

Reminder A small dialog box that displays in the middle of the Outlook screen that is used to remind you of a pending appointment or task.

Ribbon The area along the top of an Outlook form that contains frequently needed commands.

Right-click The action of clicking the right mouse button.

Root folder The first folder from which all other folders branch.

ScreenTip A small box that displays useful information when you perform various mouse actions such as pointing to screen elements or dragging.

Scrolling The action of moving a pane or window vertically (up or down) or horizontally (side to side) to bring unseen areas into view.

Server In a client/server network, the computer that manages shared network resources and provides access to the client computer when requested.

Shortcut menu A context-sensitive menu that displays commands and options relevant to the selected object.

Submenu A second-level menu activated by selecting a menu option.

Table Style A format that lists the contents of a folder on a single page and provides limited information about each item.

Task A personal or work-related activity that you want to track until it is complete.

Task Pane A pane, usually below the appointment area, that can be used to schedule tasks.

To-Do Bar A pane, usually along the right edge of the Outlook window, which provides quick access to daily tasks.

To-Do List pane A pane that displays an area to type a new task and a flag for each task.

Toolbars Rows of buttons, usually located under a menu bar, from which you can perform commands using a single click.

Views Ways to look at similar information in different formats and arrangements.

Wizard A feature in Microsoft Office programs that walks you step by step through a process.

Work week A calendar option that shows only the weekdays, Monday through Friday.

Index

SINGLE PC LICENSE AGREEMENT AND LIMITED WARRANTY